Taking Psychoanalytic and Psychometric Perspectives toward a Binocular Vision of Religion

Religion and Psychology

Volumes published in the Brill Research Perspectives title are listed at *brill.com/rpsy*

Taking Psychoanalytic and Psychometric Perspectives toward a Binocular Vision of Religion

By

Barbara Keller

BRILL

LEIDEN | BOSTON

This paperback book edition is simultaneously published as issue 2.2 (2020) of *Religion and Psychology*, DOI:10.1163/25897128-12340004.

Library of Congress Control Number: 2020906618

Typeface for the Latin, Greek, and Cyrillic scripts: "Brill". See and download: brill.com/brill-typeface.

ISBN 978-90-04-43633-6 (paperback)
ISBN 978-90-04-43634-3 (e-book)

This book is printed on acid-free paper and produced in a sustainable manner.

Contents

Taking Psychoanalytic and Psychometric Perspectives toward a Binocular Vision of Religion

Barbara Keller
Research Center for Biographical Studies in Contemporary Religion,
Bielefeld University, Germany
barbara.keller@uni-bielefeld.de

Abstract

Current psychology of religion relies mostly on quantitative psychometric approaches for the description, explanation, or prediction of religious experience and behavior, risking narrow reifications of operational definitions and neglect of individual experience. Psychoanalytic concepts are rarely addressed, due to being seen as lacking a scientific foundation, such as hypothesis testing based on large samples. Psychoanalysts have been slow to discuss religion without suspicion of pathology. Recently, psychoanalysts have broadened their empirical work and a "narrative turn" is discernible in developmental and personality psychology, allowing the inclusion of subjective perspectives. Drawing on these developments a rapprochement of psychodynamic and psychometric approaches is suggested to gain more depth of vision. Examples are given for the areas of development, personality, and psychotherapy.

Keywords

psychoanalysis – psychometrics – religious / spiritual development – religious / spiritual personality – religious styles – interdisciplinary dialogue

1 Toward a Binocular Vision of Religion

1.1 *Psychology of Religion and the Need for Depth of Vision*

What people belief in, which traditions and world views they sustain and feel sustained by matters for their personal lives, for their communities, and—nowadays more than ever—for human relations on a global scale—for better or worse. This insight has inspired interest in the psychological study of religion

 | DOI:10.1163/9789004436343_002

from its very beginning in academic psychology and in psychoanalysis and in and across different times and places. This study suggests to engage such different perspectives and to explore how combinations of different perspectives can lead to more depth of vision for the understanding of religion in its broadest sense in the lives of individuals in their social and historical environments.

A binocular vision is a metaphor taken from optics: The depth of a field, the dimensionality of objects focused on, become visible, if more than one perspective is applied. The difference of angles, lateral disparity, results in slightly different two-dimensional pictures of the same object. The combination of both makes visible that there is a third dimension, the depth of the object in focus. In the work of Wilfred Bion this has been taken even further: He uses the image of looking through a binocular microscope at different levels (Vermote, 2019, 53–54). I borrow from that, when I suggest to regard concepts and methods from academic psychology and psychoanalysis as offering complementary perspectives.

I will look into the study of developmental perspectives, of different ways of being religious, and share clinical experiences and considerations. This implies discussing nomothetic and idiothetic perspectives, which are in different ways relying on, but not coinciding with, using quantitative and qualitative data. Historical and cultural backgrounds will be included, with the intention to stimulate interest in interdisciplinary work. I use literature offering overviews, offering inter- or transdisciplinary perspectives, and (few) specifically selected studies, and draw on research in which I have been involved in as part of a research team studying religious development, or, in our more inclusive terms, the lifelong development of the symbolization of transcendence, in Germany and the US (e.g. Streib et al., 2009; Streib & Hood, 2013, 2016; Streib, Keller, Bullik, Silver & Hood, in preparation) and on my clinical experience as a licensed psychoanalyst working in the German health system. I write in my second language, drawing on translations, where possible, sometimes offering my own, to illustrate how issues are articulated in different research contexts. The quotation marks around "religion" are intended to mark and acknowledge the many ways to understand and define this concept, which is used in scientific discussion as well as in everyday language, and which has a history. While I hope to show that the study of "religion" gains depth from combining different perspectives I am aware that I offer rather spotlights on options than a comprehensive picture.

1.2 *A Fuzzy Concept with a Complex History: Spotlights from Narratology and History*

"Is defining religion even possible?", ask Hood, Hill and Spilka (2018, 8) in the recent 5th edition of their compendium "the psychology of religion" which reviews the field from a decidedly empirical perspective, and proceed to refer pragmatically to the plurality of what may be deemed religious, depending on cultural, geographical and historical context. Barrett, proponent of the multidisciplinary paradigm of "cognitive psychology of religion" (CSR), which is invested in cross-cultural work, has even asked the radical question: "Could we advance the science of religion (better) without the concept "religion"?" (Barrett, 2017). While he is worried about the scientific dignity and usefulness of the "folk concept", he seems to appreciate it as tool for "marketing our research" (Barrett, 2017, 283). Hanegraaff (2019) takes a different position and demands that after years of deconstructing "religion" it should be reconstructed, equipped with a new narrative that takes up current notions such as "experience".

Leaving aside the issue of deconstruction and construction, I suggest to look at the "folk concept" from a narratological perspective. From there, a concept can be understood as containing a "miniaturized respectively arrested" narrative (Koschorke, 2012 331). I suggest to align "folk concept" with "commonplace" concept. Koschorke (2012, 172) uses the expression "commonplace" (Gemeinplatz) in his discussion of lexical, territorial, and social mobility of concepts. He argues that the approximate (das Ungefähre), not-understanding (Nichtverstehen), reinterpretation (Umdeutung) can be resources, and function to allow communicative compromise. Such a concept may contain and combine several narratives, thus allowing diverse usage. Similar to its current complementary in the popular binary, "spirituality" (Keller, Streib & Hood, 2016), "religion" can be used as a commonplace expression, which can contain different narratives.

This popular binary for current self-identifications offers respondents the option to separate the "system" from (varieties of) experience—at least in the western part of the world which has a Christian tradition. They have been combined in titles of journals or books (Hood, Hill & Spilka, 2018, 13–15)—and it remains to be seen how still different options of labelling forms of horizontal transcendence will be included in future titles. In other parts of the world, and for other historical periods we may find material to construct other personal narratives, built around other definitions or other concepts.

From this viewpoint what Barrett complains about may be exactly what makes "religion" so useful for "marketing" the pertaining research. Precisely the lack of precision offers enough space for different narratives, with which different people are familiar or with which they identify in different ways. This in turn may motivate interest in very specific studies, which allow, at best, based on information on concepts and methods used, the reader to interpret, integrate and criticize findings reported.

Therefore, I suggest to link story with history and to include a historical perspective on the "commonplace" concept of religion and its origin. Putting the spotlight here on retrospectives of how "religion" was developed in the Western part of the world, and in a specific time means to acknowledge that in other places of the world we may find different trajectories, which may challenge as well as enrich our reflections of our own perspectives.

Literary scholar Stephen Prickett traces the shift from "religion" to "religions" in Europe. The trajectory he describes starts with a portrait of Christianity as "final and coherent Theory of Everything", which took up and integrated the literature of antiquity and thus could provide a narrative, whose "very completeness" … "by the late middle ages made the idea of an alternative story almost unthinkable" (2002, 128). Referring to the tensions involved in such an encompassing synthesis, he describes how competing narratives lead to the emergence of the plural, "religions", "first in English but within a century right across Europe" (2002, 132–133). Drawing on the historical study of Harrison (1990) he states that "the word 'religion' only acquired its modern meaning of a particular systemized code of belief and practice in England in the seventeenth century, as the breakdown of the mediaeval synthesis, and the religious upheavals of the sixteenth-century Reformation,[1] allowed people, for almost the first time, to see that more than one such system could exist. Only then could 'a religion' be perceived as one system among several, that could be studied as it were objectively, from the outside. Only then did the word acquire its plural form. In that sense, our concept of religion is itself only about 300 years old." (Prickett, 2002, 132–133). Note the emphasis on "system", "code of belief", and "practice".

"Our concept", however, getting back to the "commonplace concept", may cover very different notions and different trajectories in different European countries, and still different in the USA. In central Europe, "upheavals" like the 30 years' war resulted in Catholic and Protestant empires and principalities. For the US, Fuller asks where the history of American religion begins, and suggests, as possible answers: the arrival of the Mayflower at Plymouth Rock, the rise of Puritanism in England, the Protestant Reformation, or the Native Americans who inhabited the continent before colonization by European

1 See also Jürgen Habermas' recent discussion exploring consequences for philosophy: "We are interested in the decoupling of faith from knowledge above all with regard to a complementary philosophy which disengages from faith and which works on its problems in a scientific way, that is—independent of personal confession—in a methodical perspective of "even if there was no God"." („Uns interessiert die Entkoppelung des Glaubens vom Wissen vor allem im Hinblick auf eine komplementäre Philosophie, die sich nun ihrerseits vom Glauben löst und ihre Probleme im wissenschaftlichen Geiste, also—ungeachtet des persönlichen Bekenntnisses—in der methodischen Einstellung des „etsi non deus daretur" behandelt.") (Habermas 2019, 192).

settlers (cf. Fuller, 2013, 1), before he lays out how religion was involved in shaping life in the early colonies (Fuller, 2013, 20–34), which ties the promise of religious freedom to a history of colonization.

In Europe and years after Reformation, protestant German philosopher Schleiermacher (1799) defined "religion" as "sense and taste for the infinite" in his essay "On Religion: Speeches to its cultured despisers". With this encompassing concept he shifted the meaning of the concept from a system or tradition to individual and experience-based ways of being religious—and to a concept of religion as a personal way of relating to the transcendent—resonating with William James' later formulation, and with current conceptions of "spirituality".

The human question of religious and spiritual experience has been discussed by the founding figures of academic psychology and of psychoanalysis. How did "religion"—as system or doctrine and as transcendental experience—fare in psychoanalysis and in academic psychology?

1.3 *Psychoanalytic Perspectives*

Sigmund Freud is famous for having dismissed religion as childish consolation in the life of individuals and, on a general level, as obstacle to scientific reasoning and enlightenment. His stance was clear: The individual had to grow up and meet the challenges of life without seeking the illusory consolation of imagined parent figures. The human enterprise as a whole should follow the ideals of enlightenment and strive for scientific knowledge and truth. For Freud religion and science are opposites, and he sides with science, demanding a stoic attitude and being adamant when it comes to shifting boundaries of defining what he is up against.

Philosophers stretch the meaning of words until they retain scarcely anything of their original sense; by calling "God" some vague abstraction which they have created for themselves, they pose as deists, as believers, before the world; they may even pride themselves on having attained a higher and purer idea of God, although their God is nothing but an insubstantial shadow and no longer the mighty personality of religious doctrine. Critics persist in calling "deeply religious" a person who confesses to a sense of man's insignificance and impotence in face of the universe, although it is not this feeling that constitutes the essence of religious emotion, but rather the next step, the reaction to it, which seeks a remedy against this feeling. He who goes no further, he who humbly acquiesces in the insignificant part man plays in the universe, is, on the contrary, irreligious in the truest sense of the word. (Freud, 1927a, 28) Beit-Hallahmi (2015, 228), uses this quote to discuss the persistence of religion referring to using "spirituality" as apologetic strategy, and thus seeking to demonstrate that Freud already criticized what he perceived as unfair or imperialistic extension of the concept.

When quoting Freud in American English I necessarily draw on translations. On these, Makari notes: "The translation of psychoanalytic terms and concepts had a long history in France, America, and England, but before 1938, these translations were auxiliary and did not fundamentally alter the semantics of the field. The collapse of Austria changed that balance. When émigrés poured into Britain and America, it became critical to consider what English translations had been adopted" (Makari, 2008, 463). Makari discusses that Freud had intentionally chosen simple words for "Ich", "Es" und "Über-Ich", which might have been translated simply into "I", "It", and "Over-Ego", because he wished to offer patients a language not too removed from their experience. However, Ernest Jones and Joan Riviere preferred the more philosophical terms "Ego", "Id", and "Super-ego" (Makari, 2008, 463)—a choice that may have given psychoanalysis a more scientistic "halo" when it was received in the US.

What do psychoanalysts nowadays say about religion? That may depend on where they work and live. From a current psychoanalytical perspective, Joel Whitebook, working in the US, has recently, in the Journal "Psyche", the central German periodical for psychoanalysts, called "to the defense of secularism in psychoanalysis" (Whitebook, 2014, 1167, my translations). His concern is "a new sympathy for religion", often labelled spirituality, supported by the linguistic turn and criticisms of positivism (1171) which lead, in his view, to relativism regarding paradigms, language games, conceptual schemes (1172), implying that science no longer commands a privileged discourse, which allows to criticize "religion". He sees, referring to academic debates in the US, the project of enlightenment in danger (1173–1174). Whitebook agrees with Freud on acceptance of limitations of human life and mortality as signs of maturity. He criticizes, with Freud, religious believers as falsely claiming that the experience of the numinous depends on supernatural beings (1180). He sees Freud arguing for science as a means against human tendencies toward magical thinking and phantasies of omnipotence. He challenges the idea put forward by proponents of object relations theory (to be explained in more detail below), that religion should, drawing on Winnicott, be seen as transitional phenomenon, and God as transitional object. He argues that defenders of religion like Rizzuto (1979) and Meissner (1984) overlook that Winnicott saw the transitional object as something that is given up on the way to acceptance of reality, adulthood and maturity. However, he concedes that Freud's criticism of religion focused on content, and that Freud discounted and rejected ritual and ceremonies, rather than reflecting and theorizing on their functions (1175–1176). Conceding that it may be part of human nature to strive for magic and omnipotence and that humans may need an equivalent of religion in a secular society, he discusses that psychoanalysis might provide helpful knowledge for providing such an equivalent. I wonder if Freud would agree to soften the stoic stance he advocated and, at least according to the early testimony of some of his followers, lived?[2]

Quite differently has the relationship of psychoanalysis and religion recently been described by German psychoanalyst and theologian Herbert Will. Working in Germany, he states that the "age of worldviews" is gone, religion has lost its universal claim to truth and power, and psychoanalysis has new options to explore religion, atheism, and convictions. He suggests to put Freud's atheism in context and regards it as not so clear cut but as rather ambivalent: There is, on one side, Freud's programmatically atheist stance when he positions himself, as young medical student, on the side of science against religion in the conflict of modernity. On the other side, there is Freud's friendship and exchange of letters with protestant minister Oskar Pfister[3] and, moreover, his marriage to Martha Bernays, who came from a traditional Jewish family (see Will, 2014a, b).[4] Will discusses the implications of Freud's marriage not to a fellow atheist or critic of religion, but to a pious Jewish woman for whom it was a big concession to give up rituals like lighting the Sabbath candles. In Freud's family, after the wedding of Freud and Martha, no Jewish rituals were performed nor holidays celebrated. Rather, there were celebrations of Easter and Christmas. Freud's sons were not circumcised (Will, 2014b, 42). Martha complied as long as Freud lived. For her own funeral she planned, with her Rabbi, a religious ceremony (Will, 2014b, 73). Will interprets this as an interpersonal manifestation of Freud's conflict between a strictly scientific stance, which he openly lived and argued for, and a religious attitude, which he did not feel nor acknowledge, but which manifested itself in his loyalties and in his interest in the subject. Will claims that in the psychoanalytic tradition identification with Freud's taking sides with science led to accepting atheism as element of psychoanalytic reasoning. Here, he sees a risk of self-delusion due to lack

2 His friend and physician, Max Schur, gives an account of Freud's last moments. After a long history of cancer and some 30 operations, Freud reminded him of the promise given years earlier, that he would assist him to end his life (see Schur 1982, 592–621).

3 Pfister wrote the first textbook of psychoanalysis. Makari (2008, 304) labels it "ecumenical", and relates that it "became popular among Americans like Stanley G. Hall, who lauded the book's open discussion of the various schools that had formed in psychoanalysis".

4 See the chapter „Die zwangsbefreite Martha bleibt fromm" (Martha, forced to freedom, stays pious) in Will 2014b, (62–64, 74).

of reflection of one's own positionality, and lack of exploring the unconscious components of one's own religious *and* atheist convictions. These strong convictions have, in Will's view, a strong seductive side, which he sees reflected in the high operating temperature he ascribes to debates on religion (2014a, 26).

While in the US psychoanalysts continue to discuss Freud and his stance toward religion (e. g. Hewitt, 2014; Kenny, 2015), in other parts of the world, there is the observation of a "sea-change" of the attitude of current psychoanalysis to religion and spirituality (Simmonds, 2006). I wonder if Whitebook's agenda involves a higher "operating temperature", because he is working in a cultural surround, the US, where religion has a different history and a different—more powerful?—status compared to "eurosecular" Germany—and where the "age of worldviews" is not regarded as over? It seems that in the US positions are more adamant either in arguing for a decidedly atheist psychoanalysis, for methodological agnosticism for psychoanalysts, for mutual acceptance and understanding, or even for integrative approaches.

Rapprochement of religion and psychoanalysis in the US is not even new. Dagmar Herzog has described the rise of psychoanalysis in the US after the second world war. She traces the development of ego-psychology as presenting itself as shifting the focus from the original (or "Freudian") concern with conflicts between libido or sexuality and the demands of culture to healthy functioning according to the principle of reality. This allowed a rapprochement of this specific brand of psychoanalysis not only with psychiatry, but also with mainstream Christianity (Herzog, 2017, 21–55). The pervasive influence of psychoanalysis in postwar US, and friendly responses from religion can be illustrated with the early observations of philosopher and political activist Günther Anders, son of developmental and personality psychologists William and Clara Stern. William Stern himself had reviewed Freud's 'Interpretation of Dreams', and, while acknowledging "fine observations and theoretical perspective" finally rejected the psychoanalytic method for lack of scientific foundations (Kauders, 2014, 37, my translation). His son noted, when living as an immigrant in New York in 1949: "The analysis racket[5] here reaches unimaginable dimensions. Highest religious dignitaries strive (probably without ever having thrown a glance at "totem and taboo") to find a "common denominator" for religion and analysis. So inevitable is already (or still) the public compulsion of this movement." (Anders, 1989, 86, my translation). Interestingly, he seems to

5 Anders wrote in German, however inserting the American word "racket" which may be read as indicating his irritation.

have hinted at the possibility, that psychoanalysis would not have that prestige forever.[6]

But what do psychoanalytic perspectives on religion look like today? Psychoanalysis itself has developed since the days of Freud. The late Stephen Mitchell has summarized: "Just as physicists have changed greatly from Freud's day to ours in their understanding of material forces, so have the ways psychoanalysts understand and talk about psychodynamics. With the fading of drive metapsychology and the energic model, psychoanalysts today talk more about internal objects, self-states, representations, and internal relations among selves and objects. But the signature feature of psychoanalysis and its language remains the focus on internality, the description of conscious and unconscious subjective states" (Mitchell, 1999, 91). Expanding on Fred Pine's (1988) model of "four psychologies" I offer a synopsis in Table 1.1.

TABLE 1.1 Psychoanalytical perspectives on religion

Analytical orientation	Central concepts	Reference to religion
Drive theory	Desire and drive, defense and conflict, spiritual drive	God as parental figure, protection against breakthrough of drive
Ego psychology	Reality testing, adaptation, defense mechanisms	Faith as support / surrogate for ego-functions
Self-psychology	Boundaries, continuty, appreciation of experience of self, receptive self-objects, coherent self	Selfobject-function vs "false self"
Object relations theories	Early childhood experiences, inner objects, good, bad, and ambivalent	God representation, transitional space
Intersubjectivity / Relational perspective/ Mentalization	Recognition of others as humans with inner lives, reflectively encountering others' and one's own inner lives	Religious experience, reflected and anchored in relationality

6 In a polemic way which borders on the arrogant, Anders also ties the "analytic racket", which he sees characterized by a fixation on sexuality, to the Puritan heritage of the USA: "It can only happen to a former Puritan to turn into a professional Non-Puritan." (87).

According to the summarizing view provided by Pine's (1988) portrayal of "four psychologies", psychoanalysis can focus on drive and instinct, on taming socialization, and gratification of drives. Note, that Ostov (2007) postulates a "spiritual drive" and includes the physical dimension in his conception of religious development which he traces from early infancy to early adulthood. His account of a "developmental epigenetic scheme" of "the human-divine encounter" starts with parallels between "forms of divine service", which he understands as "efforts to make contact with the divine" and characteristics of the child's early attachment relationship to her/his mother (Ostov, 2007, 61, 67–89). Parallels between attachment and religious behaviour are located in the sensual experiences of seeing, hearing, smelling, being nourished. Ostov also explores gestures involved in religious practices and rituals, such as prayer, and relates them to parent-child-interaction. Focussing on the "spiritual" he takes a stance which acknowledges the roots in his own tradition, strives for neutrality, while being open to religious themes. Second, it can, as ego psychology, focus on the development of autonomous ego functions, controlling impulses and integrating contradictory feelings, thus supporting the adaptation to the external world (cf. Herzog, 2017, 35). Third, self-psychology aspires to understand and support the development of a differentiated and whole sense of self (Pine, 1988, 582–583). Fourth, object relations theory explores histories of inner representations of significant relationships with the aim of gaining freedom by understanding patterns no longer functional. I have added the recent relational perspectives, which include how relationships are created and understood in the therapeutic situation, and the mentalization program, which has a focus on the development of being aware of one's own and other's inner lives.

Religion can, from a drive theory perspective, provide a strong parental figure which helps to defend against breakthrough of drive. Religion can serve as support for or even as surrogate for ego functions, offering adaptive strategies. Third, self-psychology explores self-object functions and fosters an authentic self. Thus, it might be a point of departure for the function of religion as either supporting or hindering the development of an authentic self. Fourth, object relations theory explores histories of inner representations of significant relationships with the aim of gaining freedom by understanding and dissolving patterns no longer functional. Ana-Maria Rizzuto's work studies representations of the "living God" to which people relate (Rizzuto, 1979, see more below). Drawing on recent discussion on primary intersubjectivity, on attachment, mentalization, and the relational basis of understanding inner and social worlds, psychoanalysis can focus on understanding changes of individual modes of relating to the transcendent. Thus, psychoanalysis seems to have turned to the study of religion, however, from a marginalized position.

With the rise of biological models, of cognitive behavior therapy, and psychopharmacology psychoanalysis lost its privileged position in the US. In Germany, the history of psychoanalysis was dramatically marked by the rise of fascism. Until today, persons and their decisions and positions taken by the leading German psychoanalytic societies before, during, and after fascism and the second world war are subject to debate. While psychoanalysis is available as treatment in the public health system, it is not part of psychology curricula at state run universities and it remains to be seen if this will change during current reforms of psychotherapeutic training. Reservations toward psychoanalysis are usually based on notions of seeing the "talking cure" as providing entertaining stories, but no scientifically based knowledge or therapy. In light of current research (e.g. Leichsenring, Abbass, Hilsenroth, Luyten, Munder, Rabung & Steinert, 2018) as well as earlier studies (e.g. Leuzinger-Bohleber, Stuhr, Rüger & Beutel, 2003) this seems at best dated, at worst prejudice in scientific garb. Psychoanalysis being reluctant to engaging in interdisciplinary scientific dialogue and slow with efforts to demonstrate the effectiveness of its methods, may have contributed to its present precarious position with respect to academic psychology in the US and in Germany. What about religion in academic psychology?

1.4 *Academic Psychology*

William James starts the second of the famous "Gifford Lectures" with a critical discussion of options of defining the essence of "religion": "Meanwhile, the very fact that they are so many and so different from one another is enough to prove that the word "religion" cannot stand for any single principle or essence, but is rather a collective name" (James, 2012/1901–2, 29). He made a distinction, when structuring his lectures, stating: "At the outset we are struck by one great partition, which divides the religious field. On the one side of it lies institutional, on the other personal religion" (James, 2012/1901–2, 31). His subject is individual religious experience: "Religion, therefore, as I now ask you arbitrarily to take it, shall mean for us the feelings, acts, and experiences of individual men in their solitude so far as they apprehend themselves to stand in relation to whatever they consider the divine" (James, 2012/1901–2, 32). James was interested in what religion does for believers, in its functional aspects. For him, religious experience is an important aspect of being human which deserves to be studied. His position has been described as more respectful than Freud's, as pragmatic as well as functional (Hood et al., 2018, 28).

Less well known is that Sir Frederic Bartlett, famous for his studies on remembering, who can be seen as having anticipated much from the agenda of modern cognitive psychology, has also discussed religion. In his study "Religion as experience, belief and action", he critically discusses the claim of "one of the most widely known and influential of modern psychological systems" "that all forms and the original impulses of human religion can be given a complete and full causal explanation within what is called the natural order of events", and that there can be no other explanations. He objects that these claims rest on assumptions like a "natural" explanation being better than any other, which, Bartlett argues, cannot be supported by psychology alone (Bartlett, 1950, 4). He also observed that religion as belief may fluctuate: "No man believes all that he believes all the time" Bartlett (1950, 17). He sees doubt as part, not as opposite of belief. He cautions psychologists not to "take sides" when studying religion, demanding a methodologically agnostic view.

Hood, Hill & Spilka trace, in the introduction to their 2018 volume of their extensive compendium, the history of the scientific psychological study of religion as having shifted from concern with conceptual issues to empirical research—and, currently, to mainstream psychology. This implies working with "objective" methods, methods which are based on empirical data, gained by assessments relying on operationalizations, on translations of concepts into observable units of behavior or cognitions, and evaluation methods which often make use of sophisticated statistical models. This has repercussions for issues of conceptualizations of "religion" as well as "religiosity": the widespread reliance on scales assessing variables, which are then studied regarding relations and predictions may leave little room for the detailed study of individual varieties of religious experiences. Transferring Lamiell's criticism of statistical methods in mainstream psychology, a large part of empirical research in the psychology of religion could be labelled psycho-demography of religion (cf. Lamiell, 2019, 18).

Overlapping with psychological approaches is the field of "Cognitive Study of Religion" which strives to work interdisciplinary as well inclusive with respect to diverse cultures and religions, and which is committed to an evolutionary (naturalist?) perspective. In the words of one of its proponents: "If we can identify a single core assumption of CSR, it is that religious ideas are natural by-products of ordinary, universal human cognitive processes (Bering, 2006; McCauley, 2011; Xygalatas, 2016)" (Hood et al. 2018, 92). Freud might have approved. Hood et al. (2018, 35) might object: That religion is nothing but a by-product may sound reductionistic to persons who identify themselves as religious. Does this imply that to (some) religious persons the theory of evolution can be nothing more than a competing "Theory of Everything" which they cannot accept because it would threaten their religiosity? Perhaps this might be what Whitebook sees the need to fight against in the US, where the majority of the population claims to believe in (a Christian) God. Evolutionary psychology's success in providing a fuller understanding of religion and spirituality as part of the new paradigm will depend upon its openness to a truly interdisciplinary effort, including a willingness to give theology its due, state Hood et al. (2018, 506). The psychoanalytic option here might be to provide space for the exploration of conceptions as well as of underlying motives of "science first" and as well as "religion first" perspectives, and to argue for the toleration of tension—inter- as well as intraindividual. This, however, is difficult, more so, when issues of power and access to resources are involved.

The decidedly atheist stance of traditional psychoanalysis has already been mentioned, also the notion of CSR to regard religion as byproduct of evolution. Another position is to refrain from discussions of the truth of specific contents of religious traditions, in line with Bartlett's advice not to take sides, or with William James' strategy to focus on function. Hood et al. also adopt a "'methodological agnosticism,' in which transcendent realities remain as possible contributors to a full understanding of religion" (see Hood et al., 2018, 3). Other scholars take a position which explicitly puts religion first. For example, Hall states, in his article on "psychoanalysis, attachment, and spirituality", when introducing the attachment system: "God designed this system to motivate infants to stay physically close to their caregivers, and to establish communication with them" (Hall, 2007, 22). I would call him an apologetic, as in his integration of psychoanalysis and religion the latter is clearly privileged—and the assumption of an evolutionary origin of attachment, as put forward by Bowlby (e.g. Bowlby, 1969), challenged.

This might look reductive, if not unscientific, to proponents of the theory of evolution, which may be acceptable to Hall. It demonstrates that, in a globalizing world with different world views, agreement on basic assumptions can be problematic. For scientific dialogue on the functions of the attachment system it might be regarded as less relevant if the creation of attachment is attributed to evolutionary processes or of divine design. Thus the methodologically agnostic view might be preferred for pragmatic reasons. From a psychoanalytic perspective this affords to live with open questions and tolerate tension.

Perhaps surprising in light of the engagement of the founding figures in psychology and psychoanalysis, and in light of increasing doubts regarding the secularization is the considerable neglect of religion as field of study in academic psychology and in psychoanalysis. "Religion" is rarely discussed in psychological textbooks. In Germany, psychology of religion is not part of the academic curriculum in psychology. Rather, it is taught in contexts of religious studies or in theology departments, as part of religious education or pastoral care. In curricula of psychoanalytic training "religion" is also rarely found. For psychotherapy in general in Germany Hoffmann and Walach (2011, 84) observed, based on their representative survey: "A total of 66.5% of the psychotherapeutic practitioners asserted that clinically relevant questions related to spirituality/religion should be given more regard in graduate education. In all 81.1% of them reported that such issues were rarely or never discussed in psychotherapy training." Hoffmann and Walach also report, that cognitive-behavioral and psychodynamic therapists found spirituality or religion less important than integrative and humanistic therapists.

For the US, Sorenson (2004, 71) has noted a "blind spot" in psychoanalytic training. This seems to point to a gap between curricula and interest of students and practitioners. However, Lev has recently drawn a more optimistic picture: "The positive relation to the religious and the spiritual is still at the margins of psychoanalytic practice and thought—but these margins are gradually getting broader, and their contents are seeping into the mainstream (Lev, 2018, 43)." And for psychology in the US, Aten, O'Grady and Worthington (2011) report even a "boom", stating that religion and spirituality "are no longer on the fringe or considered taboo in the larger field of psychology" (2). This view would have to be complemented by findings from other places in the world, including diverse historical perspectives.[7]

1.5 *Studying a Fuzzy Concept*

Religion has been portrayed as fuzzy from the outset, covering traditional beliefs and values as well as highly idiosyncratic experience. Consequently, Hood et al. (2018) point to the problems involved and take the pragmatic approach of briefly reviewing the five major world religions with the aim to capture those characteristics which are most likely relevant to psychological functioning (Hood et al., 2018, 9). Discussing spirituality versus religion, they suggest that spirituality may overlap with horizontal (privatized, experience-oriented) transcendence, religion with vertical (tradition-bound, institutionally mediated) transcendence (Hood et al., 2018, 14–16, see also Streib & Hood, 2013).

7 See for example Jensen (2019) who studies "How the couch got to Calcutta", comparing the parallel developments of early psychoanalytical organizations in Berlin, London and Calcutta, noting that Freud's criticisms of religion were discussed in these three cities and thus in different religious contexts (Jensen 2019, 311).

Whatever the stance taken, it is important to attend to definitions offered. Hood et al. (2018, 39) state: "Any attempt to measure a concept such as religiousness or spirituality requires that the concept be specified in measurable terms. Such an "operational definition" is especially important when applied to religiousness and spirituality, because ... there is considerable variety in how these terms are conceptualized". This refers, for example, to self-report scales or observational measures. Thus, the operational definition, which specifies, how the construct is put to work empirically, gives it a precision, which a definition grounded in knowledge and semantics, cannot offer. To rely on a supposed common notion can lead to misunderstanding as can be shown from the reception of research in which I have been involved: "Notably, the use of faith development interviews to gather qualitative data on all aspects of a person's faith is problematic when applied to non-religious people. For example, a cross-cultural study on deconversion conducted by Streib et al. (2009) found that participants who opted for non-religious worldviews were assigned even higher stages of faith than religious people. Given that atheism is characterized by the absence of faith (Altemeyer and Hunsberger, 1997), it appears counterintuitive to state that those who identified as non-religious had a sense of faith more developed than religious persons themselves. It certainly seems that Streib et al. (2009) have conflated theology with social science bringing theological concepts into research that is arguably psychological in nature (Gooren, 2011)." (Pérez & Vallières, 2019, 3).

What puzzles the authors can be clarified by realizing that Streib et al. worked from a broad concept of "faith" which includes what some respondents described as "spiritual", based on James Fowler's encompassing definition (see below), and on a methodology, which allows the description of subjective forms of faith. Subjective varieties of faith are not captured by broad categories like "religious" or "non-religious", which, although widely used in self-report scales, carry different meanings and connotations for different people.

This points to the challenges of interdisciplinary work which hinges on efforts at understanding concepts across disciplines. "Translations" and "back-translations" may involve attention to the "biographies" of concepts, which have a historical as well as a disciplinary context. The reflection of those heritages might protect against discipline-specific reifications. It should also support reflections on how to identify and use converging perspectives to formulate research questions and how to choose and implement empirical methods to collect the data on which an answer can be based.

1.6 *Different Research Methods, Different Levels of Analysis*

Turning to methods, it looks promising that in recent decades academic psychology has seen an opening toward narrative and autobiographical methods (see Schiff, 2014 and his references to Cohler's (1982) seminal chapter for a retrospective). Schiff notes that "narrative is able to "personalize" developmental knowledge. As a part of psychological science, developmental psychology strives to account for generalizations beyond the persons being studied." Referring to Lamiell's criticism (see more below), Schiff contends that based on psychometric methods "knowledge of the average" is taken for "knowledge of the general" (Schiff, 2014, 10). He reasons that by "systematic description of how and why differences are realized" a narrative perspective can help to understand how individuals understand, and by using their reflection, shape their development (Schiff, 2014, 10–11).

This may indicate a connectivity to the "talking cure". Psychoanalytic researchers have traditionally worked with protocols of what is narrated and communicated in treatment sessions, ideally to be written down after the session, and to integrate and condense clinical experience toward vignettes or case studies. Freud wrote about his own that they "read like novellas" and "lack the serious stamp of science" (Freud 1895, 160). Within psychoanalysis, a turn to observation occurred when Bowlby started to use direct observation of interaction with caretakers as method for the study of early relationships, and not childrens' unconscious phantasies or reconstructions of early experience on the couch, decades later. This was first received with harsh criticism and caused controversy (see below). Meanwhile, observation has gained acceptance, the study of infants and young children also, and tapes and transcripts are used for inquiries of communication and language and how they are used in the therapeutic process (see e.g. Kächele, Albani & Pokorny, 2015).

There have been major changes in the psychoanalytic study of development and of treatment: While the case study is still an important form of discussing therapeutic strategies, in recent years psychoanalysts have appropriated strategies of quantifying observations. Psychoanalysts have also turned to study the effects of their interventions, including quantitative and psychometric methods in their designs of therapy processes, and outcomes. They have moved from "novellas" to diagrams of statistical analyses, from reliance on idiographic to inclusion of nomothetic methods. What does this mean? We take a look into the history of psychological research:

For personality and differential psychology Lamiell (2019, 32), has critiqued how supposedly objective methods are used in psychology. He draws on the classics of the field and reports: "Allport borrowed the terms 'nomothetic' and 'idiographic' from the German philosopher Wilhelm Windelband (1848–1915), who used them not as labels for two contrasting methods for personality research, but rather to name two different kinds of scientific knowledge. One kind, the 'nomothetic,' takes the form of general laws on the model of the *natural* sciences (*die Naturwissenschaften*), i.e., laws in terms of which to *explain*, as Windelband himself put things, *that, which always is* (in German: *das, was immer ist*) in some particular domain of empirical investigation. The other kind of knowledge, the 'idiographic,' consists of contextually meaningful accounts of non-recurrent happenings or entities on the model of the *human* sciences (*die Geisteswissenschaften*), providing, in any given instance, an *understanding* of what has been, or of *what once was* (in German: *das, was einmal war*) in a given domain of investigation (cf. Windelband, 1894/1998)" (Lamiell, 2019, 32).

Lamiell discusses Windelband's early efforts to describe psychology as an empirical science, which strives for idiographic *and* nomothetic knowledge (Lamiell, 2019, 167). He argues for a "revival of a broader vision of the discipline as a science, a vision that, as a matter of historical fact, once prevailed" (Lamiell, 2019, 168). I see his suggestion to turn to an "idiothetic" approach as strategy not only to remedy misinterpretations of statistics, but also to attend to a richer variety for the study of human experience:

> With the neologism 'idiothetic,' I sought to identify an approach to personality studies whereby the determination of those traits relevant to the description of any given individual's personality would be done idiographically, i.e., case by individual case, 'nomothetic' knowledge would be found, if at all, in what might prove common to all in the domain of personality development" (Lamiell, 2019, 32). Thus, the study of the individual might even come first, and based on the study of individual cases—what once was—, commonalities—that which always is—could be assessed. Already in 1981 he had laid out in detail: "Programmatic research of the type just described would be idiographic in the sense that it would be predicated on an idiographic measurement rationale and would literally involve the study of single individuals over time. It would also be nomothetic, however, in that it would seek to confirm, across individuals, the applicability of certain basic principles to an understanding of theoretically relevant phenomena. In a word, the research would be idiothetic. (Lamiell, 1981, 286)

Lamiell argues for diligent work with scientific data and their interpretation: "The argument is that in order to defend the claim that one is studying empirically the degree of consistency with which particular attributes are manifested by individuals, one must at the very least be dealing with empirical findings that are both (a) relevant to the question of (in)consistency and (b) interpretable at the level of the individual." (Lamiell, 1987, 106). Lamiell draws on the work of William Stern, the German developmental and personality psychologist, who had developed the "intelligence quotient", and who was mentioned above as father of Günther Anders. He sympathizes with Stern's plea for careful methodological work and for attending to difference understood as human individuality. I read Lamiell's criticism also as encouraging the combination of different methods with different strengths. The challenge then may be how to develop measures which can be used in diverse settings and contexts, doing justice to the particulars, and methods to integrate results which can be communicated and compared beyond the site of data collection? This depends on the types of instruments and on how instruments are set to work. In the psychology of religion there has been the call for measures, which capture the specifics of cultural and religious context beyond Western Christian cultures. Hood et al., for example, recommend: "It is important that we recognize the limits of our measures and seek to improve them for more diverse settings" (Hood et al., 2018, 41). Ağılkaya-Şahin has discussed the implications of this ambition for the psychology of religion in Turkey, attending to intricate problems of translation not only of items of psychometric measures or of interview questions, but also of central psychological and religious concepts (Ağılkaya-Şahin, 2015).[8]

There are measures which claim cross-cultural applicability. For example, the items of Hood's Mysticism scale (see below) offer respondents basic descriptions of how mystic experiences feel and asks to rate the extent of familiarity with each experience. How the items are best structured according to the overarching dimensions of extrovertive, introvertive, and vertical mysticism / interpretation, can differ for different cultural contexts (see, for example: Chen, Hood, Yang & Watson, 2011). Analyses suggest that there is a cross-cultural common core based on experience, while the way, basic experience is structured, may differ.

A different method, the Faith Development Interview, explores religious experience as embedded in biography: covering the domains life review, relationships, values and commitments and religion and word view, it is used in different cultural contexts (Streib & Keller, 2018, Tarar, Hassan & Keller, 2017,

8 Above I have noted this challenge for the translation of vocabulary of psychoanalysis from German to English. Here, I add that Jensen extends the question of translation to discussions in Calcutta, where glossaries of basic concepts in Bengali were compiled by the first non-western psychoanalytical association (Jensen 2019, 123–127).

Aygün, 2010, Özışık, 2015, Butenaite, 2019). Important is the focus on experience, either assessed or reported.

The nomothetic-idiothetic distinction cuts across different levels of measurement: McAdams distinguishes in his research program between dispositional traits, characteristic adaptations, and life narratives, or the study of the person regarding supposedly universal traits, motivations, and biographies (McAdams & Olson, 2010). Dispositional traits are broad internal dimensions of personality thought to account for general consistencies in behavior, thought, and feeling observed across situations, such as the "Big Five": five broad factors repeatedly derived from factor-analytic studies of traits: extraversion, neuroticism, openness to experience, agreeableness, and conscientiousness (e.g. Costa & McCrae, 1985, McCrae & Costa, 1987). Characteristic adaptations refer to goals, plans, projects, values, possible selves, and other contextualized features of personality capturing individual differences in motivation, usually assessed with specific psychometric scales (McAdams & Olson, 2010, 519). Narrative identity means an internalized and evolving life story that a person begins to develop in late adolescence to provide life with meaning and purpose (McAdams & Olson, 2010, 527).

In the psychoanalytic study of religion, narrative data are used and narrative identity is addressed. In psychoanalytic treatment the aim is to achieve change toward more health or maturity—and interpretations are structured according to the specific psychology used or question addressed. I will use different types of data and different levels of description as well as different psychoanalytic psychologies in the following chapters for discussions of the study of religious experience in development, personality, and therapy.

2 What Develops in Religious Development?

Human lives develop, situated in specific historical times, with their respective cultural, political, and religious surrounds. This affects also scientific efforts, basic concepts and instruments involved, as well as basic attitudes. Development of religion in phylogenetic perspective is today a subject discussed by CSR. The ontogenetic development of religion is explored in religious education and pastoral psychology, in psychoanalysis, and, although less than might be expected, in developmental psychology. The focus will be on psychoanalytic and attachment approaches, which, so far, have offered the most elaborate accounts of developmental trajectories and mechanisms.

Textbooks on developmental psychology offer scarce information on religious development. For the study of human development in academic psychology Bloom (2007) accounts for the lack of studies of religious development with a taboo (Bloom, 2007, 148): "Once we put aside its taboo nature, religion can be studied in the same way as any subfield of developmental psychology." With Freud, who also discussed taboo, however in a different sense, he shares, across the time of a century, a critical perspective, from which religion is seen as less than rational—and rather not developed. Freud was concerned about animism, belief in magic, and the "omnipotence of thoughts", drawing, in "Totem and taboo", parallels between "the Mental Lives of Savages and Neurotics", (Freud, 1913/1919). Freud works with a developmental model, which he applies to phylogenesis and to ontogenesis, and which consists of three "great world systems": the animistic (mythological), the religious, and the scientific. Badcock (1980) has provided the most sophisticated defense of Freud's phylogenetic theory from within psychoanalysis.

However, Freud's phylogenetic speculations have been widely criticized by those otherwise sympathetic to Freud's speculations (Grünbaum, 1984, 1987; Meissner, 1984; Shafranske, 1995; Hood, 1997). Hood et al. give historical background: "The Latin-derived term "animism" was introduced into anthropology by Edward Burnett Tylor in 1866." He defined it "as a minimum definition of Religion, the belief in spiritual beings." Animism is then said to be "the deep-lying doctrine of Spiritual Beings" (Tylor, 1873, 72–73). It also includes the belief that inanimate things possess life or spirit, even intention and motive. Its origins were first assigned to prehistoric peoples once labeled "primitive savages" (Hopkins, 1923, 11). Modern psychology rejects such verbal chauvinism." (Hood et al., 2018, 63). Bloom, in contemporary vocabulary, discusses cognitive bias: "The proposal here is that there are certain early-emerging cognitive biases that give rise to religious belief. These include body—soul dualism and a hyper-sensitivity to signs of agency and design. These biases make it natural to believe in Gods and spirits, in an afterlife, and in the divine creation of the universe. These are the seeds from which religion grows" (Bloom, 2007, 150).

Freud and Bloom discuss, in different (original) languages and different vocabularies, characteristics of thinking not yet fully developed, for example, the tendency to distinguish between body and souls, which opens the option to think that there can be souls without body. See, for example, Freud, 1919, chapter 3: "Human beings have souls which can leave their habitation and enter into other beings; these souls are the bearers of spiritual activities and are, to a certain extent, independent of the 'bodies'." Bloom, 2007, 149: "If bodies and souls are thought to be separate, you can have one without the other. Most things, such as chairs, cups, and trees, are thought of as bodies without souls, not possessing goals, beliefs, will, or consciousness. More significant for religion, dualism makes it possible to imagine souls without bodies." Freud would expect the "savages" to develop toward more civilization and to discard religion in favor of scientific thinking, and the neurotics, to gain insight and let go of immature illusions. Bloom seems to rely on cognitive development, which leads to scientific thinking. Both, however, concede that "religion" may have some function. Both views, while formulated more than 100 years distant from each other, might impress apologetics of religion as reductionist.

Their views will be complemented by agnostic perspectives from current psychoanalysis, from attachment theory in developmental psychology, and then mentalization will be discussed as concept with potential toward integrative perspectives. First I attend to object relations theory and to Rizzuto's work on the development of the "Living God", which takes a careful reconstruction of "Freud's implicit theory of object representation" as point of departure (Rizzuto, 1979, 29). I then engage with the late Stephen Mitchell's model of different modes of interaction (Mitchell, 2000), because it offers a typological as well as developmental perspective for structuring observations of relating—to persons as well as to the transcendent (cf. Keller, 2008).

2.1 *Object Relations and the Living God: Ana-Maria Rizzuto*

Ana-Maria Rizzuto has offered an object-relations account of religious development. Her approach is discussed here because it has been influential for modelling faith development to be introduced below. Also, it can be seen as a "prototype" of an object relations perspective on religious development as well as of a psychoanalytic attitude toward handling religiosity in therapy (see chapter 3). She traces the development of the God representation as a special type of object representation, which is created first in the transitional space (Winnicott, 1953), and then, across the life span, transformed according to life phases and developmental tasks (Rizzuto, 1979, 206–207). She claims, relying on the exploration of childhood as remembered, that children create their object representations of God in the transitional space, an area of illusion and play, which is essential for human development (Rizzuto, 1979, 73). Based on her clinical studies, she identified four positions taken in relation to God: 1. There are "those who have a God whose existence they do not doubt; 2. Those wondering whether or not to believe in a God they are not sure exists; 3. those amazed, angered, or quietly surprised to see others deeply invested in a God who does not interest them; 4. those who struggle with a demanding, harsh God they would like to get rid of if they were not convinced of his existence and power" (Rizzuto, 1979, 91). From her psychoanalytic object relations perspective she assumes that the primary objects, such as parents, provided most of the characteristics of a God representation. She is interested in the elaborations and transformations such parentally inspired representations have undergone, in exploring psychic defenses which might facilitate or prevent belief, in life conditions and traumas which also influenced the development of the God representation, and in the use a person makes of their private God, and the needs in relation to that God. Then, she is interested in the relation of the private God and the God provided by organized religion (Rizzuto, 1979, 91). These questions guide her elaborate case studies, which are based on retrospective interviews with adults.

2.2 *Psychoanalysis, Relational: Increasingly Complex Interactions*

A different view on development has been offered by Stephen Mitchell (2000). He has suggested a hierarchy of four modes of interaction according to their onset and complexity. Mode 1 refers to non-reflective behavior, to patterns of reciprocal influence, "to what people do with each other" (Mitchell, 2000, 58). In Mode 1 others participate in recurrent, often stabilizing patterns of interaction. Referring to attachment theory, these are traced to early "instinctive activities, such as sucking, clinging, and smiling" (60), physical activities not yet symbolized nor reflected upon. Mode 2 is concerned with affective permeability, that is, with direct affect resonances between people, with empathy. "Mode 2 is shared experience of intense affect across permeable boundaries" (58) In Mode 2, others participate in affective connections. Mode 3 is "experience organized into self-other-configurations" (58), the self is shaped by different relationships and in relation to different others. In Mode 3, distinct others are symbolized, but play specific functional roles. Mode 4 means intersubjectivity, that is, mutual recognition as subjects; self-reflective intentionality and dependency. In Mode 4 others are organized as distinct subjects (Mitchell, 2000, 58–62). The hierarchy of these modes corresponds to the sequence of their onset. These modes have been used for an understanding of faith across the life span (Keller, 2008), assuming that, after onset, they continue to develop, not necessarily balanced, and more or less in interaction with each other. The earlier modes of presymbolic interaction and transpersonal affect will persist, and so will, throughout life, bodily sensations as a quality of which persons are more or less aware. Acknowledging the permanence and importance of earlier forms of inner life, Mitchell adds functionality to complexity. He refers to Loewald (1978, 31) who suggested that "The richer a person's mental life is, the more he experiences on several levels of mentation, the more translation occurs back and forth between unconscious and conscious experience. To make the unconscious conscious is one-sided. It is the transference between them that makes a human life, that makes life human" (Mitchell, 2000, 152, endnote 7 to chapter 2). However, the tensions between hierarchy, complexity and integration as markers of development deserve further study. Autobiography, life review, can be used as windows on the processes involved. According to this conception, the relationship to the transcendent or to God would be expected to develop from reciprocal influence and regulation to presymbolic interactions across mutually shared experience to dialogical forms, keeping earlier modes and thus providing a typology covering a developmentally ordered range of options of relating toward whatever someone perceives as transcendent. This is different for the attachment perspective, which focusses on mechanisms of transmission of "internal working models". The contribution of attachment theory to the psychology of religion is discussed in the next paragraph.

2.3 *Attachment and Religious Development*

Attachment theory is based on the studies of John Bowlby, a British psychoanalyst. It was further developed by Mary Ainsworth, who designed the "strange situation" for the study of children, and Mary Main, who developed the Adult Attachment Interview (AAI). Kirkpatrick (1992) transferred it to the study of religion. Recent research has established that individual differences in attachment have important implications for religious development and especially for a person's perceived relationship with God (Kirkpatrick, 2005) or, presumably, the transcendent.

From an attachment perspective religious development (Granqvist, 2010, Granqvist & Kirkpatrick, 2016, 932ff) has been discussed as structured according to a compensation or a correspondence pathway. Compensation means that in the case of parental insensitivity and insecure attachment, a perceived relationship with God helps to regulate a believer's distress when confronted with attachment system (hyper)activation, and when no other options are available (Granqvist & Kirkpatrick, 2016, 925–926, see also the respective chapters in Granqvist, 2020). Correspondence means, that the religious beliefs and behaviors of people who are securely attached can be expected in part to reflect their sensitive parent's religious standards. Granqvist and Kirkpatrick (2016, 928) note that the impact of parental religiousness is moderated by the quality of the relationship between child and parent.

Further, Granqvist has proposed a mediational model in which disorganized attachment (including unresolved loss or abuse) is hypothesized to predict altered spiritual states, via dissociation (e.g., absorption) as a mediating variable (Granqvist, lvarsson, et al., 2007), both with mystical experiences (Granqvist, Hagekull, & lvarsson, 2012) and New Age spirituality (Granqvist, Fransson, & Hagekull, 2009) as outcomes, predicted by unresolved loss or abuse (Granqvist & Kirkpatrick 2016, 927, see chapter 8 in Granqvist 2020 for recent extensions). The import of attachment theory to the psychology of religion has resulted in robust findings—and inspired the revival of an old conflict with psychoanalysis.

2.4 *Psychoanalysis and Attachment: a History of "Bad Blood"—and Reconciliation?*

Psychoanalysis and attachment theory share a complicated history. Bowlby was trained at the British Psychoanalytic Institute, while he studied medicine and psychiatry. His training analyst was Joan Riviere, and Melanie Klein herself supervised his early clinical work. Inge Bretherton, who gives an account on the origins of attachment research, relates how conflict arose, when Bowlby wished to talk to the mother of a child he treated under Klein's supervision. He was convinced that early experience was important—and that treatment could not be based on attending to unconscious phantasy alone (Bretherton, 1992). Bretherton also notes, that Bowlby responded with formulating his own research ideas (Bowlby, 1940). His ideas were neither welcomed by the Kleinians, nor by the Freudians. Mitchell quotes Grotstein (1990, 62) stating "that the virtual expulsion of Bowlby from psychoanalysis" was "one of the most dreadful, shameful and regrettable chapters in the history of psychoanalysis" (Mitchell, 1999, 90).

Meanwhile, there is rapprochement of psychoanalysis and attachment. Fonagy and his team have, with the concept of mentalization (see below), participated in creating dialogue and collaboration. Fonagy and Campbell testify: "In all, however, it would be fair to say that the growing dominance of a relational and relationship-focused emphasis in 'modern' psychoanalysis over recent decades has resulted in an increasing implicit interest in objective observations concerning the formative nature of the child's social environment, and the emergence of object relations theory as the 'lingua franca' of modern psychoanalysis has played a pivotal role in this context". (Fonagy & Campbell, 2015, 230). What the attachment perspective shares with the object relations approach is the idea that we constantly form and elaborate inner ideas, pictures, of the relationships we live with. In the language of object relations we create representations, in the language of attachment theory we create inner working models from our experience and according to our specific ways of perceiving and processing information.

Fonagy and Campbell elaborate: "The study of attachment-related narratives was accepted as providing a window on the internal working model (IWM) (Bretherton and Munholland, 2008). This once again brought attachment theorists into a common domain of theoretical and clinical discourse with psychoanalysts writing from an object relations perspective. In essence, the 'operationalization' of IWMs, as 'structured processes' (Main, Kaplan &

Cassidy, 1985; Main, Hesse & Hesse, 2011), allowed attachment theory to accommodate greater human complexity, fluidity and subjectivity than was expressed in the reflexive, Pavlovian behaviours that early psychoanalytic critiques attributed to attachment-based interpretations." (Fonagy & Campbell, 2015, 231).

This relaxed attitude was not directly transferred to the psychology of religion. Rather, inspiring associations of the return of the repressed, the conflict between attachment and psychoanalysis was restaged in the psychology of religion. Granqvist, researcher on attachment in the psychology of religion, criticized the "Depth"-Approaches (Granqvist, 2006), which were defended by Rizzuto (2006) and Wulff (2006). This debate was summarized by Luyten and Corveleyn (2007). In their view there is a larger issue to discuss: "What is really at stake is a discussion about the opposition between two cultures in the social sciences in general and the psychology of religion in particular (see also Hood & Belzen, 2005): one more interpretive, the other built on the model of the natural sciences." (Luyten & Corveleyn, 2007, 90). Instead of supporting a dichotomic perspective they suggest to attend to methodological varieties *within* the different camps. Conceding that there are sociocultural, institutional, power, and personal issues involved, they encourage to dare explore each other's worlds. In terms of methods, they refer, among other options, to nomothetic-idiographic-nomothetic research cycles (Luyten & Corveleyn, 2007, 92). Their suggestions regarding design seem to resonate with calls for mixed-methods-approaches, for careful monitoring of what happens on different levels of analysis during research processes, and with Lamiell's longstanding admonitions to clearly distinguish between data based on explorations of groups or individuals. Granqvist has recently looked back on the controversy and its aftermath, not sparing his own involvement. His critical review will hopefully inspire, for reflection of scientific socializations and developments, what psychoanalysts are famous for demanding: remembering and working through (Granqvist, 2020, 265–267). Next, the concept of mentalization will be discussed as integrative option, linking attachment, cognitive development, and psychoanalysis.

2.5 *Mentalization as Integrative Concept for the Psychology of Religion?*

The concept of mentalization is portrayed here in more detail, because of its potential for the study of religious development (cf. Keller & Streib, 2013). Also, it allows an illustration of methodological variety in terms of operationalization of a concept: There is the option of using, based on clinical observation, the descriptions of the trajectory of pre-mentalizing (teleological, psychic equivalence, pretend mode) to mentalizing states like a typology. The Reflective

Functioning Scale, based on ratings of the Adult Attachment Interview, offers a continuous measure, based on quantified qualitative data. More recently, the Reflective Functioning Questionnaire (RFQ) was published (Fonagy P, Luyten P, Moulton-Perkins A, Lee Y W, Warren F, Howard S, et al., 2016), a self-report measure, an "objective" scale, which offers options for predefined responses to be counted, that is, quantified.

Mentalization has been defined as the capacity to envision and think about mental states, in oneself and in others, in the service of building realistic models of why they behave, think, and feel as they do (see Fonagy & Target, 1997, 679). Mentalization understood in this encompassing way is more than theory of mind. It has been described as resting on three research traditions: Theory of mind, attachment theory, and psychoanalysis.

Theory of mind in cognitive developmental psychology explores the development of taking over others' perspectives in terms of the information they have available. In the well-known "Maxi"-experiment a child is asked to construct what a person in a story is likely to know: Maxi and another character start from shared knowledge regarding where a piece of chocolate is stored. Maxi leaves the scene and the other person puts the chocolate into a different place. The question is, where will Maxi look for chocolate when he returns? Most children below age 4 will give their answer according to where the object has been moved to, relying on "reality", while most six-year-old children take into account that Maxi was not present while this happened and answer based on what knowledge they theorize as available to Maxi (Wimmer & Perner, 1983).

Attachment theory has discovered that a haven of safety or a secure base serves as point of departure and as place of safe return for the preschool child exploring his or her environment. This perspective stresses the affective conditions of exploration and cognitive development and thinking. Alluding to Winnicott's 1971 work "Playing and reality", Fonagy and Target have presented mentalization as result of "playing with reality". Winnicott (1971, 15) saw the "intermediate area" as offering relief from the ongoing task of reality acceptance and as the origin of arts and religion. In the conception of Fonagy and Target mentalization develops as the child learns, protected by secure attachment, to move back and forth between pretend play and reality, that there is something like an inner life.

The third tradition implied is psychoanalysis: "The psychoanalytic process is the arena par excellence for studying the underlying psychic activities which enter into the organization, maintenance, and growth of the individual mind" (Loewald, 1970, 61, cited in Allen, Fonagy, and Bateman, 2008, 8). This refers to inchoate experiences, feelings of tension, for example, which need to be noted and "digested" in order to be processed as feelings. By guiding the child toward processing impressions into words and concepts early caregivers support the development of symbolic function. "The mother approaches the crying baby with a question in her mind: "Do you want your nappy changed?" The sensitive caregiver can bridge the focus on physical reality and internal state, sufficiently for the child to identify contingencies between them (Fonagy & Target, 2003, 273)." Learning about one's own and others' inner life is, from the beginning, anchored in relationships. A closer look at the developmental trajectory introduces the different modes of perceiving inner and outer world which are involved. Target and Fonagy stress the central role of early relationships. In their view the child is not "an isolated processor of information, engaged in a construction of a theory of mind from first principles accumulating representations of the world from observation" (1996, 461). Rather, development of mentalization can be regarded as relational theory of achieving symbolization:

Between birth and 5 months, interactions of infant and caregiver can be described as presymbolic (emphasis added), not mentalized: "the infant is not required to represent the thoughts or feelings of the caregiver" (Fonagy, Gergely, Jurist & Target, 2002, 32). Drawing on research by Gergely and others they suggest that "by the second half of the first year infants' perception of social contingencies is "*teleological*" in that they make reference to future states (goals) as entities in the interpretation of behavior based on the principal of "rational action"" (Fonagy et al., 2002, 33, italics original). Fonagy (2008, 26) states that the child "is simply judging rational behaviour in terms of the physical constraints that prevail and that which is obvious in terms of the physical end state which the object has reached". It is argued that the development from teleological to mentalizing models depends on the quality of interpersonal interactions between the infant and the caregiver.

The child's early subjectivity is characterized by psychic equivalence as mode of experiencing. Inner and outer reality are not yet separated, but presumably experienced as just "reality". Affect congruent, contingent and marked mirroring helps the child to learn about the difference between representational and actual mental states (Fonagy & Target, 2003, 274). Marked mirroring refers to a response which validates the child's experience, mirroring by repeating the child's utterance, while also communicating, usually by slightly exaggerating, that one is responding to the child's inner state from one's own perspective. Marked mirroring can be combined with naming what is perceived: "Oh, how sad! Do you want a hug?" Thus, children may learn that what they feel is sadness and that this can be understood and dealt with. Marked mirroring takes up inchoate experience and makes it mentally manageable by providing it with words, thus supporting symbolization.

Pretend play, usually emerging in children's third year, is supposed to foster the understanding of mental states. "Pretending requires a mental stance involving the *symbolic* (emphasis added) transformation of reality in the presence of, and with a view to, the mind of the other" (Fonagy et al., 2002, 47). Secure attachment supports the child's moving between phantasy and reality. "The adult, ... holds the frame of external reality while accurately representing the child's mental state" (Fonagy et al., 2002, 48). The young heroes, involved in staging their adventures, rely on their parents to call them to dinner, while they are immersed in their dramas. As a second prerequisite the authors name talking, pointing to "evidence that conversations about feelings and reasons behind people's actions are linked to relatively early achievement of reflective function" (Fonagy et al., 2002, 48). Also, pretend play and playfulness provide a space for the child to explore and exercise ways of functioning which are developmentally advanced. Play seems to encourage progress.

At around 4 years children start to integrate psychic equivalence and pretend mode toward mentalization. Moving away from the separation of equivalent and pretend mode requires the prior development of a healthy core self. The child's perception of mental states in himself and others depends on observation of the mental world of their caregiver, thus, mentalization has an interpersonal and a self-reflective component (Fonagy & Target, 2003), which are in interaction. The child, increasingly aware of an inner life, by which experience is mediated, is increasingly able to predict what others may do and to manage his or her own feelings. A clearer representation of others' minds supports communication and deepens intersubjectivity (Target & Fonagy, 1996, 462–463).

Mentalization is a concept that can help to understand the development of symbolization. It is also helpful for the understanding of communication. The recent integration of "epistemic trust" in the mentalization framework could also be of interest for the psychology of religion, as it is about depending on care-givers, who transmit social knowledge to the next generation. The right amount of epistemic trust—between believing too easily nor not believing anything at all—is crucial for growing into and then getting along in a complex social world. Moreover, just as attachment, epistemic trust might be explored to better understand what and how—and perhaps whom—humans believe, when they construct their religion or world view.

Recently, Fonagy and colleagues have taken the argument one step further. They suggest to regard "epistemic trust" as "another important function of attachment relationships", which serves the transmission of cultural knowledge across generations (Fonagy & Campbell, 2015, 239): "In our view, the major evolutionary advantage of attachment in humans is the opportunity it gives the infant to develop social understanding. According to this evolutionary perspective, a particular attachment style could be seen less as a measurement of the extent to which the parent was able to succeed in generating infant attachment security. The attachment style adopted by the child should, more broadly, be seen as an adaptive learning outcome concerning what might be the most appropriate method for social survival in a complex interpersonal world" (Fonagy & Campbell, 2015, 241). The authors contend "that even serious personality disorders such as borderline personality disorder (BPD), while conspicuously dysfunctional in our normative social setting, may have adaptive benefits for individuals living in an emergency milieu characterized by high levels of interpersonal violence, where there is a need for extreme vigilance on issues of self-protection and where there is significant benefit in being able to form intense emotional relationships, which might elicit critical protection or resource supply very quickly" (Fonagy & Campbell, 2015, 241).

The concept "epistemic trust" is used in literatures from cognitive across educational to clinical developmental psychology which focus on different aspects: selective trust, different learning and natural pedagogy, and the role of (early) attachment relationships in the ability to trust. It is the latter I want to explore.

Here is a current definition: "Put briefly, the theory of epistemic trust posits that the human infant—most usually first within the context of early attachment relationships—is instinctively inclined to develop openness to the reception of social communications from their primary care-givers. Stated otherwise, epistemic trust is an adaptation allowing the infant to receive social knowledge from their better-informed elders, enabling them to benefit from the complex edifice of human knowledge that their immediate culture has available to them." (Fonagy, Luyten, Allison & Campbell, 2017). The authors point out that under challenging conditions epistemic trust will develop in a way which is adaptive and functional under these circumstances: "In situations where a young learner's early environment is heavily populated by unreliable communicators, the opening of epistemic trust becomes problematic: it may be more adaptive to remain persistently vigilant about, or even closed off to, the communication of social knowledge. In the face of an abusive and hostile caregiver, whose intentions towards the infant or child are not benign, epistemic mistrust becomes entrenched as an appropriate adaptation that has been prepared by natural selection."

The implication is, however, that under different conditions this behavior may become problematic. Epistemic vigilance and mistrust may then be met with irritation. Also, it is possible that persons feel safe in environments which validate their epistemic notions. This might allow a reconstructions of the psychoanalytic repetition compulsion in attachment-based terminology: People might gravitate toward behavior that inspires others to meet their expectations.

Here might, in the field of psychology of religion, be an opportunity to link different, however related, approaches and to turn to what Granqvist and Kirkpatrick have observed from their attachment perspective: "Of course, the appeal of the New Age for disorganized individuals may also be due, in part, to its provision of metaphysical affirmations of these individuals' psychological states and experiences (e.g., of telepathy, contact with the dead, possession by abusive perpetrators). Prior to the individuals' introduction to the New Age, such states and experiences may well have been regarded, by self and others alike, as worrisome signs of poor reality contact." (Granqvist & Kirkpatrick, 2016, 297). New Age options may—like other religious or world view options—offer something like a "cultural container" (Will, 2017), providing an inner space in which individual experience can be held, felt, and put into words.[9] New Age may provide pictures and communicable vocabulary for otherwise inchoate inner states. The research of Granqvist and Kirkpatrick may be read as pointing to the downside of unreflective turns to such containers, which may foreclose usage of other options.

Object relations theory has offered accounts of individual development, which have been useful for therapeutic assessment and structuring treatment. Given their retrospective nature, however, Granqvist is still right, when he misses methods on which to base predictions. Similarly, Mitchell's model offers therapeutic orientation and an interesting heuristic for the inclusion of spiritual or religious issues in treatment. While attachment research offers a reliable empirical methodology on which it can base predictions, Granqvist concedes: "the attachment framework remains somewhat schematic and impoverished as applied at the individual level" (Granqvist, 2020, 267).

This calls for deliberations on how to study individual appropriations of transcendence and their development in a way which attends to individual, and elaborated in further steps, general trajectories. Next, hybrid models of

---

9 I draw here, again, on the work of Herbert Will. He introduces this concept in his analysis of poems Edith Jacobson wrote in Nazi detention. The German psychoanalyst from an assimilated Jewish family had been arrested because she had supported a socialist resistance group. In prison she uses impressions from pictures by Fra Angelico, friar and renaissance artist in Florence, to contain her extreme experience. Will describes a process of transgression from inner need, across delimitation of the self and search for vitalization of a religious world toward an experience of redemption. He suggests to regard religious traditions as cultural containers, which can support transformation of individual experience—even of "nonreligious" persons, who are, like Jacobson, reflective and aware of what they are doing (Will 2017).

religious development are reviewed. The following models can be seen as interdisciplinary hybrids, as models consisting of elements of theories and of concepts from different disciplines. The first reviewed is James Fowler's conceptualization of "stages of Faith" (Fowler, 1981), to be followed by Heinz Streib's program of the religious styles (Streib, 2001).

2.6 *James Fowler: Faith Develops across the Life Span*

James Fowler was a Methodist theologian and professor of Theology and Human Development. In his modelling of the "stages of faith" he combined theological and psychological theories and concepts. In his 1981 book he gave an encompassing definition for "faith". Referring to Cantwell Smith (1963; 1979), he defined 'faith' not as religion in the sense of cumulative traditions (institutions, texts, religious traditions) nor as belief, in the sense of consent to the content of certain ideas and symbol systems. In basic agreement with Cantwell Smith, Fowler (1981, 92–93) defined 'faith' as a person's constructions and reconstructions of everyday experience in light of the ultimate conditions of existence, thus as ways of meaning-making in response to transcendent centers of value and power. Fowler's conceptualization of 'faith' is very broad, open and inclusive—capturing a kind of "common core" of various religious and worldview traditions, embracing theistic and non-theistic worldviews, and also ways of meaning-making which do not refer to any religious tradition.

Another inventive idea Fowler's was his conception of development of faith across the life span, which resonates with the concept of life span development put forward during the 70ies of the last century. Fowler proposed that "faith", understood in this encompassing sense, and not tied to content of a specific tradition, does develop across the life span. Therefore, he strived to distinguish between content and structure, and sought to study structural change. Fowler built on Piaget, understanding religious development to be structured by the development of cognitive competences. In Fowler's model, however, Piaget's stage conceptions are stretched: Departing from Piaget's conception of cognitive development, which arrives at its final stage in young adulthood, faith development is assumed to cover the whole life span. Formal operations, in Piaget's conception the end point of cognitive development and tied to the acquisition of systematic scientific reasoning in (young) adulthood stretch from stage 3 (early formal operations) across stage 4 (formal operations, dichotomizing) to stage 5 (formal operations, dialectical) and stage 6 (formal operations, synthetic) (see Fowler, 1981, 244–245). These "stretched" stages of cognitive development are assumed to develop from young adulthood far into adulthood. Aligning Piaget's model of cognitive development to life span models of his time in a trajectory toward an ideal informed by his Christian

Methodist orientation Fowler proposed that psychological and theological perspectives coincide.

He presented his integrative adaptation of structural accounts of cognitive development toward a theory of faith development across the life span, spanning 7 "aspects" also named "windows on faith": cognitive development (drawn from Piaget), role taking (Selman), moral reasoning (Kohlberg), adding bounds of social awareness, locus of authority, forms of world coherence, and level of symbolic functioning. These seven aspects of faith are assumed to develop across six stages: Intuitive-projective (<6 years): The person at this stage is assumed to be unable to distinguish readily between fantasy and reality, or to differentiate between the object and the way it appears to him or her. The world is comprised in part by numinous projections and fantasy, it is magical and unpredictable. There is little ability to take the perspective of the other. During the next stage, mythic-literal (7–12 years), the person is a young empiricist, interested in concrete links between things and events. They have become more concrete and realistic and project themselves into myths and stories. There is little notion of the interiority of the other. The third, the synthetic-conventional stage (adolescence, adulthood) is characterized by concrete others and interpersonal harmony. There is a felt sense of the attitudes and opinions of others, a more abstract valuing of relationship for its own sake. The self is not apt to differentiate itself from the relationships in which it is engaged. Its identity is a derived identity. Individuative-reflective faith, stage 4 (adulthood) is described as autonomous, the self at this stage as distinct and self-conscious entity. Drawing on Erikson, stage 4 faith is described as characteristically ideological, a time of attempting to work out one's philosophy of life, of concern with self-definition and boundary maintenance. Stage 5, conjunctive faith is dialogical, there is an increased emphasis on human subjectivity and the need for individual decision-making in the face of an ambiguous reality, an increased awareness of the historical and temporal nature of understanding, while claims of self, family and one's own group can still exert a powerful influence upon the individual. This is less important for universalizing faith, the last stage 6, which is related to an all-encompassing ideal or vision of the good that is indicative of a sense of relationship to and participation in the whole of our totality of being. Fowler's model has been validated based on cross-sectional data from 359 interviews covering an age range of 3.5 to 84 years, by demonstrating a correlation of the stages with age (Fowler, 1981, 318).

In later texts Fowler expanded the scope of his interdisciplinary efforts at anchoring faith development and presented summary descriptions with interpretations in terms of Kegan's (1982) Evolving Self, or in categories of modernization and postmodern life and with respect to infancy research (Stern, 1985) and Rizzuto's (1979) psychoanalytic view of the development of God representations (Fowler, 1987, Fowler, 1996, see Streib, 2011, 2). Fowler himself seems to have situated his project in terms of alignment with then current reasoning: "The author of Faith Development Theory grew up in an era when liberalization of religious traditions seemed to be the apparent path toward keeping religion current with modernity" (Fowler, 2004, 418).

2.7 *Criticism and Revision: Heinz Streib's Religious Styles Perspective*

From the beginning Fowler's program has met criticism as well as support, and Heinz Streib has offered both, critiquing and refining the development of faith development theory and research. He has reconstructed Fowler's project as an "ambitious search for a combined structural-developmental and liberal-theological plausibility" which, however, "is … not without tension" (Streib, 2011, 1).

Heinz Streib's earlier criticisms of Fowler's approach focussed on the neglect of the autobiographically situated self with its affects and emotions in religious development, drawing on Gil Noam's criticism: "It is my view that cognitively based theorists have overlooked the central structuring activities of the self by defining the epistemic self as the sole representative of structure. In the process, I believe, the cart was placed before the horse, life history became content to the structure of the epistemic self … Epistemology replaced life history." (Noam, 1990, 378, quoted in Streib, 2001, 144). In more detail, he criticized the neglect of the psychodynamical and relational interpersonal dimensions; of the interpretative, hermeneutic dimension, and of the life-world dimension (Streib, 2001, 144). He suggested to draw on the philosophical (phenomenological) contributions of Maurice Merleau-Ponty (1988), and Paul Ricoeur (1990) to situate faith development in the life worlds of persons. Moreover, he referred to the psychoanalytical and psychological contributions of Erik Erikson (1968), Ana-Maria Rizzuto (1979) and Gil Noam (1990) to account for the dynamics of individual developmental trajectories (Streib, 2001, 145–147), highlighting the importance of the study of narrative and narrative integration of experience for faith development research (148).

The religious styles perspective (Streib, 2001; 2003; 2005; 2013, Streib & Keller, 2018, Streib, Chen & Hood, 2019) has been elaborated as result of critical-constructive engagement with Fowler's project and is conversant with new concepts and research methods in developmental and personality psychology. It opens up perspectives of flexibility and permeability of religious styles, rather than confining "development" to the sequential abandonment of stages that are considered structural wholes. The term "style" is in the new manual (Streib & Keller, 2018) used to avoid fixation to a linear, irreversible developmental model and to open the perspective on the multi-directionality and diversity of developmental trajectories. This resonates with current reasoning in developmental psychology, where the life span perspective has gained acceptance (Baltes, Lindenberger & Staudinger, 2006).

The styles still describe a hierarchy but are depicted with more openness and flexibility. They are assumed to emerge corresponding to a developmental sequence. However, individual trajectories across the lifespan may differ, not necessarily covering the entire spectrum of styles, and develop multi-directional (moving "upwards" or "downwards" in the hierarchy). Aspect-specific profiles calculated from manual-based FDI evaluation show that it is the rule rather than the exception that more than one style is simultaneously available for a person at a certain time. Attention to combinations of different styles for different aspects or in different domains thus allows the portrayal of intra-individual variety.

The joint (if not conscious) presence of different developmental levels belongs to the foundations of psychoanalysis. Freud had compared the city of Rome with its layers of historical remnants to the human psyche to illustrate that there are deeper and older levels of inner life, that besides current development earlier stages continue to exist (Freud, 1930, 18). This bears similarity to Streib's model of the religious styles, which appear, one after the other, and layer upon layer, allowing for the reappearance of earlier and less refined forms of faith, for "heterodyning", elements of different styles to appear in combination. There is hierarchy (from early to late, from basic to advanced, from simple to complex), but no insistence on linear trajectories. Rather, these illustrations allow for different configurations of cognitive, affective and emotional development and call for an inspection of integrative models from current psychology.

The main difference, however, between Streib's descriptions of the different religious styles and the descriptions of the stages of faith in Fowler's writings is a new focus on inter-personal relations. This is, in the recent new edition of the "Manual for the Assessment of Religious Styles in Faith Development Interviews" (Streib & Keller, 2018) reflected in the labels for the religious styles and revision of the aspects. "Perspective Taking" is presented as initial aspect, while "Form of Logic", based on Piaget's structural theory of cognitive development, has been discarded. Thereby, the religious styles perspective puts stronger emphasis on the life-world, life-history and inter-personal world of the individual, departing from the overemphasis on the epistemic self in Fowler's work. Structures are now defined as patterns of cognitive and affective operation by which content is understood, expressed, and transformed. How these structures can be accounted for by specific developmental and differential assumptions is the aim of empirical inquiry.

Another change was dropping stage/style 6, which Fowler labelled Universalizing Faith. The conceptual reason for this is grounded in interdisciplinary and interreligious acceptability: a psychologically plausible model of religious styles need not and should not be based on, teleological and theological (eschatological) propositions, which Fowler (1981) described with the theological metaphor of the Kingdom of God. The religious styles perspective thus consists of the subjective, instrumental-reciprocal, mutual, individuative reflective, and dialogic style, which can be substantiated by empirical research.

They can be roughly aligned to related concepts as suggested in Table 2.1. There, the stages are presented on one side of the spectrum, as the model that makes the most definite assumptions (linear upward succession of defined stages, development structured by "form of logic" or cognitive development sensu Fowler's appropriation of Piaget's work). Rizzuto's model focusses, from a psychoanalytic object relations perspective, on one domain of religious experience, on the development of the God representation and the pertaining relationship to whatever someone regards as their God. Fowler (1981, 108) and Rizzuto (1979, 206–207) refer to Erikson's model of developmental tasks, tying development to the sequence rendered in his conception of the life span. Erikson's model, however, has been labelled soft, because he did not postulate that stages be discarded. Rather, he assumed, that the respective developmental tasks are likely to be in the foreground in the life period assigned. Styles, modes of interaction and modes of pre-mentalizing to mentalizing ways of perceiving self and others are assumed to appear in a hierarchical sequence in childhood, but then develop further dependent on and as part of complex interactions with social conditions. These conceptions also imply multidirectionality and multidimensionality, based on an interactive understanding of cognition and emotion, embedded in experience, as motors of development. Thus, we see different conceptions of development as hierarchical and/or functional displayed.

The hybrid models put forward by Fowler and Streib have been described and aligned to the models of Rizzuto, Mitchell, and the mentalization approach of Fonagy and Target. This allows to inspect parallels of descriptions of stages, styles, and modes—of relating to "faith" or generally, to some "other". Also, it allows to inspect different developmental assumptions from strong stages (when a new stage is entered, the preceding is discarded) across "soft" stage conceptions (stages follow each other, but more in the way of shifting priorities of developmental tasks), to styles and modes (there is a sequences

TABLE 2.1 Stages, styles, representations, and modes of interaction and symbolization: Parallels between the models discussed

Fowler 1981: Stages of faith (hard stages)	**Rizzuto 1979: God representation (soft stages)**	**Streib 2001: Religious styles (sequences of occurrence and hierarchy)**	**Mitchell 2000: Modes of interaction (complex interactions)**	**Fonagy and Target 1997: Mentalization (modes)**
Intuitive-projective faith				Teleological mode, presymbolic
Mythic-literal faith	Aggrandized parental images	Instrumental-reciprocal or "do-ut-des" style	Nonreflective behavior: behavioral patterns of interaction, reciprocal influence	Psychic equivalence—perception = reality
Synthetic-conventional	God as a personal partner	Mutual style	Affective Permeability: direct affect resonances between people	Pretend mode: discovering inner worlds
Individuative-reflective faith	Emotional distance from representations, critical assessment, relatedness and trust in deeper layers of the psyche	Individuative-systemic style	Self-Other-configurations: organized co-constructed interactions	Integrating psychic equivalence and inner worlds toward ...
Conjunctive faith	Uncertainty about and questioning of God representations, presentiment of presence of trustworthy other, emergence of basic trust	Dialogical style	Intersubjectivity: mutual recognition as subjects; self-reflective intentionality and dependency	... Mentalization: own and other's inner worlds and intentions

of occurrence and hierarchy), founded on philosophical reasoning (religious styles) or developmental plausibility and oberservation (modes of interaction, modes of more or less mentalization). Thus, the table also illustrates a tension between more normative and more adaptive or functional conceptions of development. Aware of this tension, the next chapter turns to recent innovations—and to methods and instruments.

2.8 *Focus on Experience and Biography: The M-Scale and the Faith Development Interview*

Streib's engagement with faith development theory has, in longitudinal collaboration with Ralph Hood, evolved into a research program which keeps developing. Basic components are the focus on religion / worldview as anchored in experience and biography, the turn to a longitudinal perspective, and, recently, the exploration of changes in responding to the 'Strange' as related to development in matters religious or transcendental. The research program has its focus on religion as lived and experienced. In terms of methods, it strives to work with a "common core" while also attending to the particulars of religious experiences, biographies, and trajectories in changing and diverse religious landscapes.

Hood's Mysticism Scale (see Table 2.2) has been shown to capture, in Western societies with Christian traditions, what is labelled "spirituality". There, "spirituality" refers to individualized experience-orientated religiosity. The M-scale can assess spirituality of a diversity of participants who affiliate with various religious traditions and worldviews, including the non-religious, atheists and non-theist, in other words, capturing vertical as well as horizontal transcendence (Streib, Klein, Keller & Hood, in press).

TABLE 2.2 Hood's M-Scale, its long and *short* version.

1.	*I have had an experience which was both timeless and spaceless.*
2.	I have never had an experience which was incapable of being expressed in words.
3.	*I have had an experience in which something greater than myself seemed to absorb me.*
4.	I have an experience in which everything seemed to disappear from my mind until I was conscious of only a void.
5.	I have experienced profound joy.
6.	I have never had an experience in which I felt myself to be absorbed as one with all things.
7.	I have never experienced a perfectly peaceful state.
8.	I have never had an experience in which I felt as if all things were alive.

TABLE 2.2 Hood's M-Scale, its long and *short* version. (*cont.*)

9. I have never had an experience which seemed holy to me.
10. I have never had an experience in which all things seemed to be aware.
11. I have had an experience in which I had no sense of time or space.
12. *I have had an experience in which I realized the oneness of myself with all things.*
13. *I have had an experience in which a new view of reality was revealed to me.*
14. I have never experienced anything to be divine.
15. I have never had an experience in which time and space were non-existent.
16. I have never experienced anything that I could call ultimate reality.
17. I have had an experience in which ultimate reality was revealed to me.
18. *I have had an experience in which I felt that all was perfection at the time.*
19. I have had experience in which I felt everything to be part of the same whole.
20. *I have had an experience which I knew to be sacred.*
21. I have never had an experience which I was unable to express adequately through language.
22. I have had an experience which left me with a feeling of awe.
23. I have never had an experience which was impossible to communicate.
24. I have never had an experience in which my own self seemed to merge into something greater.
25. I have had never had an experience which left me with a feeling of wonder.
26. I have never had an experience in which deeper aspects of reality were revealed to me.
27. I have never had an experience in which time, place and distance were meaningless.
28. I have had an experience in which I became aware of unity to all things.
29. *I have had an experience in which all things seemed to be conscious.*
30. I have never had an experience in which all things seemed to be unified into a single whole.
31. I have had an experience in which I felt nothing is ever really dead.
32. *I have had an experience which cannot be expressed in words.*

These items tap into experiences, which can be familiar to people holding various religious and non-religious world views. On the group level, the observations can be structured accordingly, resulting in slightly differing factor solutions.

Similarly, the Faith Development Interview has been used with persons from different religious and non-religious world views (see Table 2.3). It seems to tap into something which can be studied across cultures, as it does, in the interview, allow to attend to specifics of a given life story in a given social and historical context, and moreover: in interviews respondents can talk back and comment on the questions they receive.

TABLE 2.3 The Faith Development Interview (cf. Streib & Keller 2018)

Life review

1. **Reflecting on your life thus far, identify its major chapters**. If your life were a book, how would you name the different chapters? What marker events stand out as especially important?
2. **Are there past relationships that have been important to your development as a person?**
3. **Do you recall any changes in relationships that have had a significant impact on your life or your way of thinking about things?**
4. **How has your world view changed across your life's chapters?** How has this affected your image of God or of the Divine, or what is holy for you? What does it mean to you now?
5. **Have you had moments of intense joy or breakthrough experiences—moments that have affirmed or changed your sense of life's meaning?**
6. **Have you experienced times of crisis or suffering in your life?** Have you experienced times when you felt profound disillusionment, or that life had no meaning?—What happened to you at these times?—How have these experiences affected you?

Relationships

7. **Focusing now on the present, how would you describe your parents? How do you see your current relationship to them?** Have there been any changes in your perceptions of your parents over the years? If so, what caused the change?
8. **Are there any other relationships that are important to you?**
9. **What groups, institutions, or causes, do you identify with?** Why are they important to you? Are there groups that have been important to you, but are not important anymore? Did you leave a (religious) community recently?

Present values and commitments

10. **Do you feel that your life has meaning at present?** What makes your life meaningful to you?
11. **If you could change one thing about yourself or your life, what would you most want to change?**
12. **Are there any beliefs, values, or commitments that seem important to your life right now?**
13. **When or where do you find yourself most in communion or harmony with the Universe?**

TABLE 2.3 The Faith Development Interview (*cont.*)

14. **What do you consider mature faith or a mature way to handle existential questions?**
15. **When you have an important decision to make, how do you generally go about making it?** Can you give me an example? If you have a very difficult problem to solve, to whom or what would you look for guidance?
16. **Do you think that actions can be right or wrong?** If so, what makes an action right in your opinion?
17. **Are there certain actions or types of actions that are always right under any circumstances?** Are there certain moral opinions that you think everyone should agree on?

Religion and world view

18. **Do you think that human life has a purpose?**—If so, what is it? Are we affected by a power or powers beyond our control?
19. **What does death mean to you?** What happens to us when we die?
20. **Do you consider yourself a religious, spiritual or faithful person?** Or would you prefer another description? What does it mean to you?
21. **Do you pray, meditate, or perform any other spiritual practice?**
22. **Are there any religious, spiritual or other ideas, symbols or rituals that are important to you, or have been important to you?** If so, what are they and what makes them important?
23. **What is sin, to your understanding?**
24. **How do you explain the presence of evil in our world?**
25. **If people disagree about issues of world view or religion, how can such conflicts be resolved?**

With its four sections live review, relationships, present values and commitments, and religion and world view this semi-structured interview invites autobiographical remembering and reasoning. Compared to the interview schedule of McAdams (see below) it explicitly invites reflection of biographical experience, of religious concepts and identifications, and of existential issues such as death and dying. Structural evaluation starts with rating the answers to the 25 question. Style assignment frequency based on answers to the 25 questions is used for calculations of types (Streib, Chen & Hood, 2019). This strategy can be seen as quantification of qualitative data, making it compatible with psychometric measures for analyses based on large samples and subsamples. Stage aspect profiles are used for case studies, for visualizing multidimensional descriptions of faith styles and for monitoring longitudinal change in individual configurations of aspects. Consequently, this strategy is currently used in first longitudinal case studies.

Both instruments have evolved to "backbones" of a mixed methods research design for the longitudinal study of religious development. In this design, the study of religious development is based on the observation of development rather than on retrospective reports alone. Repeated retrospectives are studied together with other measures, which are followed. For example, it is possible to follow individual trajectories across several points in time for longitudinal case studies. On the basis of ratings of many interviews, that is, quantifying narrative data on the group level, types for identification of 'movers' and 'stayers' can be identified in longitudinal perspective, as currently explored by Streib Chen and Hood (2019). Thus, it is possible to monitor changing versions of religious biographies in the context of carefully chosen variables, and to make predictions on different levels of analysis. Lived religion is located in time, referring to the human life span, and to the social and historical contexts of human lives.

Since the time of Fowler's writing at least in Western industrialized societies the human life span has gained in length. This has led to clumsy psychological labels such as 'young old' and 'old old', to describe the years from the sixties onward. Colleagues of the study of religion from sociology note a surprising lack of research interest for those years. Krause ponders: "William James is widely regarded as one of the greatest psychologists of religion. Writing in 1902 he maintained that, "the religious age par excellence would seem to be old age" (James, 1902/1997, 37). This statement, coupled with a considerable amount of subsequent work, has led a number of investigators to argue that people tend to become more deeply involved in religion as they grow older. Although this perspective makes an important statement about human development, it is surprising to find that it is often overlooked in developmental psychology texts" (Krause, 2016, 264). Krause consequently points to the necessity to study change in religiosity across old age, because this covers a period from 65 to 100, and it is highly unlikely that nothing changes across 35 years (Krause, 2016, 266). In the following section we turn to this phase of life, illustrated by a case study from the deconversion project, which has been extended to a longitudinal perspective and "deconversion revisited" (Streib, Keller, Bullik, Silver, & Hood, in preparation). It follows one individual across time, and could thus be described as psychography (Stern, 1911, quoted in Lamiell, 2019, 54) or, more conventional, as idiographic. Turning to the level of the larger project which includes the use of general principles (for example, taken from the study of narratives) for the study of single cases, teasing out strategies to generalize findings, it can, following Lamiell's longstanding suggestion (see Lamiell, 2019, 32) be labelled "idiothetic".

2.9 *Former Catholic Sophia at Young Old and Old Old Age in Germany*

The case study which is used here for illustration is described in more detail by Bullik, Keller and Swanson (in preparation), based on consecutive interviews with the Faith Development Interview. Sophia is a woman from Germany who was 63 and retired at the time of her first interview for the original study on deconversion in 2004, and 72 years old at the second interview in 2013. Sophia was born during the second World War, in Upper Silesia, then part of Germany. Her family fled to the Western part of what was to become postwar West Germany, when she was a child (see Table 2.4). She has distanced herself from the Catholic Church and considers herself a deconvert. She tells, in both interviews, what made her move away from the church. However, this story changes (see tables 2.5 and 2.6), and the general way she looks back on her life does also change. She looks back, in both interviews, on her strict religious upbringing, on conflicts with her parents, on her unhappy marriage which she ended by divorce, on her relationships with her daughter and her former husband, also her friendships and her professional life. Important shifts concern how she looks back on her parents, which are portrayed in a milder light in the second interview, and how she contextualizes her life, giving, at the second interview, much more historical background, putting her life into a wider perspective.

TABLE 2.4 Social and historical contexts of Faith Development—"what once was"

Dates	German History	Sophia's life phases
1933	Hitler comes to Power	
1939–45	Worldwar W II	* Sophia 1941
Postwar years	"Refugees" from the Eastern Parts of former Germany	Childhood
1961	Labour recruitment agreement with Turkey	
1961	Pill available	
1968	Pope Paul's Enzyclical Humanae Vitae Rejection of most forms of birth control	Young adult
1968	Student protests, oppositional movement („APO")	
1977	Reform of domestic law, a married woman can have a job without her husband's consent	
1989	German reunification	Midlife
2004		Young old First interview
2013		Approaching „Old old" Second interview

For the identification of narratives, we use the structure identified by Labov and Waletzky (1967), which is used in narrative developmental research. Table 2.5 illustrates the structure of such a story, according to Labov and Waletzky, modified by Habermas and Berger (2011). Some stories in the FDI present experiences deemed meaningful regarding respondents' religious/ spiritual developments and are seen as displaying their narrative identity. We have, in earlier research, suggested calling them "religious identity narratives" (Keller, Coleman, & Silver, 2016, 253).

TABLE 2.5 Structure of narratives

Orientation	Provides background such as antecedents, place, time, and persons
Complication	Central event that breaks with normality, elicits an emotion, defines a goal
Evaluation/Attempts to solve	Assessment of the situation / Attempts to return the situation to normal
Resolution	Successful or not successful result of attempts to solve complication / adjust evaluation
Coda	Signals end, leads back to the present

When working in longitudinal perspective, we first explore if there are such small narratives and then if a narrative is reappearing in the second interview. Sophia tells in her first interview the story of her deconversion, a religious identity narrative that is taken up again in the second interview. This allows us to explore how Sophia's views on the experience involved have changed (cf. Josselson, 2009). For an illustration of the method, see Table 2.5 and the discussion below, for more details on this specific case, more details will be presented in Bullik et al. (in preparation).

While the first narrative accounts for her breaking away from the Catholic Church, the second shows her transformation from victim to victor: In the second narrative, she portrays herself as a person who stands up against the authority of the church, even if this has considerable physical consequences, and as a person who claims her own position, being in charge of the situation. Sophia presents herself in a different way, claims a different and more assertive self in the second interview. From the religious styles perspective she shows movement from a predominantly individuative-systemic to a more dialogical style. Thus, we can state progress in hierarchy as well as in functionality, as Sophia can accept herself and others better at the time of the second

TABLE 2.6 Tracing change based on religious identity narratives: Sophia 2004 and 2013

Structure	2004 / Age 63	2013 / Age 72
Orientation	In hospital, back from intensive care and recovering from blood transfusions	More detail on context, her medical condition
Complication	Visit by Catholic priest, who interprets her illness as God's punishment for her divorce. She responds with physical breakdown	Talks back to the Catholic priest; then has a breakdown
Evaluation/ Attempt at solution	She discusses her acceptance of "God's judgment" with a doctor who reassures her and suggests to send for protestant minister	Doctor announces to send for female protestant minister who will surely be supportive
Resolution	Female protestant minister offers understanding both for interviewees reaction and decision to terminate her marriage	Elaborate account of minister's helpful comments, which support her life decisions
Coda	Breaking away from the Catholic Church	Account of recovery, later complaint about priest to the hospital staff

interview. Although she has discarded the Catholic faith of her childhood as narrow-minded and restrictive, she has developed her personal faith toward a horizontal transcendence, that includes the "presentiment of presence of a trustworthy other" (Rizzuto) that for her, is nature:

> I'm not religious, in no way spiritual. Neither faithful, in the Christian sense, but in a scientific sense perhaps, only that term doesn't exist there. Because I can grasp nature. Right? I can only repeat that I'm very conscious that I'm alive.

This is manifested by her care and concern for the environment as well as by the trust and self-acceptance she displays in the second interview.

3 Differential Perspectives

Academic psychology of religion also studies different ways of being religious, and more recently, of being non-religious or atheist. The latter might sound counter-intuitive, however, people also differ in what and how they do not believe (Keller et al., 2018). Here, we enter the territory of differential and personality psychology, offering two comparisons. First, we look at two case studies from the research program of Dan McAdams, then at two case studies from the deconversion project. The current study of personality does not rely on tests alone, as the research program of Dan McAdams testifies. He has suggested to distinguish between three different levels of description which we describe here in more detail:

3.1 *Attending to Difference: Different Levels of Description*

McAdams and Olson (2010) distinguish three developmental layers of psychological individuality: Dispositional traits (the person as actor), characteristic adaptations (the person as agent), and integrative life narratives (the person as author). "Personality traits sketch a dispositional outline of psychological individuality; adaptations fill in the motivational and social-cognitive details; and life stories speak to the full meaning of the individual life." (McAdams & Olson, 2010, 519). There, they also define the "Idiographic case study: the study of the individual case in personality psychology, with the goal of understanding a particular life in depth". However, the scientific co-creation of individual biography is a complex process, demanding careful handling and documentation of method, for example the interview schedule, as well as further steps of such as transcription and interpretation. To qualify as idiothetic, a strategy of working from the individual toward the general—not to be equated with the average—would be needed (cf. Lamiell).

With psychometric scales, also a lot depends on the instrument offered, but also on how it is understood. While psychologists usually hope to capture, with the scale they create, as good as possible the degree to which a person is characterized by the variable under study, there are important caveats:

One concerns what Norbert Schwarz found, when he studied how respondents construct the research interest they meet. They use the "informative functions of response alternatives" provided by response scales (Schwarz & Hippler, 1987). This means that respondents make their guesses regarding researchers' cartography of the religious field. Consequently, they try to find out where they fit best, instead of reporting what they "truly" think or feel. We have, in our research, the chance to look into that, when we compare how participants answer the question of their religious self-identification as forced choice four-option question, as continuous measure asking how "spiritual" they are, regardless of how religious or else they are, and how they answer the question in the interview, where they are allowed to use their own words and explain their understandings of the concepts.

Lamiell, again drawing on the work of William Stern, offers a critical perspective from earlier discussion in the history of psychology, quoting from a report Stern wrote about a visit to the US: "The face of American psychology is characterized much less by laboratory experimentation than by testing procedures ... Since the (First World) War, during which the entire American army was tested by means of a simple, standardized procedure for measuring intelligence, testing methods have been extended in ways that are astounding and almost troubling ... Seventeen years ago, when I introduced the concept of the 'intelligence quotient' as a measurement principle for such intelligence tests, I had no idea that the 'IQ' would become a kind of worldwide formula and one of the most frequently encountered expressions in American technical jargon ... But beyond that, batteries of tests for countless other psychological functions such as spatial perception, manual dexterity, attention, suggestibility, knowledge, arithmetic ability, character traits, etc. have now been developed, standardized, and put into use ... always with emphasis on the objective, quantitative norm, with reference to which the single case is then compared. At times, the primary objective in America seems to be to exercise technique, to obtain numerical measures which can be correlated and statistically analyzed. (What is clear) in all of this is the danger of a mechanization, ... and it is to be hoped that the zenith of the testing culture will soon be a thing of the past. (Stern, 1930, 50–51, parentheses added)" (Lamiell, 2019, 70). The concern is with the neglect of the person and their individual experience.

When compiling results from different levels of data analysis, it is important to be aware of what the methods involved can carry in terms of interpretation: Regarding the first level of personality traits, Hood et al. (2018) discuss Saroglou's explorations of the Big Five model and report that he found, across many studies "a fairly consistent pattern" (Hood et al., 2018, 254): Openness is most consistently unrelated or negatively related to religion, while agreeableness and conscientiousness are positively related to religion (Saroglou, 2002a). Also, religious fundamentalism tends to be negatively correlated with openness (Saroglou, 2002b). They suggest, as an explanation, a higher-order two-factor solution to the five-factor model measure. "Agreeableness, conscientiousness, and emotional stability (neuroticism reverse-scored) form one factor associated with stability, and openness and extroversion form another factor associated with plasticity (DeYoung, 2006; DeYoung, Peterson, & Higgins, 2002)." These findings, based on group level analyses, describe relations between variables, they do not inform about individual profiles of traits.

In the following sections I discuss what in the terminology of Stern (1911) and resurrected by Lamiell (2019) can be described as comparative research (Lamiell, 2019, 54): comparisons of single cases, first of two women in the US, who live in different religious communities, thus this is a comparison across religious communities. The cases are taken from McAdams' research. The next comparison involves the "same" religious community, Jehova's witnesses, however, in two different countries: One of the two men is from the US, one from Germany, with a history of leaving Jehova's witnesses. These cases are taken from the Bielefeld-Chattanooga-based deconversion study. For these latter cases I can draw on the Big Five and Ryff's scales on eudaimonic well being along with interview data, for the cases from McAdams laboratory I rely on the published analyses of interviews and measures of generativity and of religiosity, such as fundamentalism.

3.2 *Different Protestant Trajectories toward Redemptive Selves and Generativity: McAdams and Albaugh's Exploration of Americans in Midlife*

Autobiographical narratives have gained scientific dignity in the research program of Dan McAdams, who explores life stories and personal myths as windows on personality and identity and their development (McAdams, 1993, McAdams & Olson, 2010). McAdams has used his approach which "combines quantitative social science with the more interpretive, hermeneutical modes of inquiry that are featured in the narrative study of lives" (McAdams & Albaugh, 2008a, 255) for a contribution to the psychology of religion. This includes adapting his life story method to study differences in personality and religiosity, based on narrative analyses. Together with Albaugh he has explored religious persons and their generativity at midlife (McAdams & Albaugh, 2008a). From their sample of diverse religious orientations (Protestant evangelicals, members of Protestant mainline congregations, Catholics, and members of African-American Christian congregations) they report two case studies and thus compare how an evangelic and a mainline Christian protestant woman at midlife look upon their lives. The interview covers life story, religious faith / spirituality, and politics (see Table 3.1), overlapping in parts with the Faith Development Interview described above.

TABLE 3.1 Outline of the Faith, Politics, and the Life Story Interview (cf. McAdams & Albaugh, 2008a, 261)

Part One. The Life Story: Eight Key Scenes
- High Point (peak experience)
- Low Point (nadir experience)
- Turning Point
- Positive Childhood Scene
- Negative Childhood Scene
- Important Adolescent Scene
- Important Adult Scene
- Imagined Future Scene

Part Two. Religious Faith, Spirituality
- Overall religious orientation, beliefs, and values in a nutshell
- Religious practices
- Prayer
- Three key scenes in the Faith Story
- 1. Opening scene (an episode that connects to beginning of faith story)
- 2. Faith high point (peak experience in faith/religion/spirituality)
- 3. Faith low point (nadir experience in faith/religion/spirituality)
- Change and continuity in religious beliefs and practices over time
- Alternative Story: What if you had no religious faith?
- Other

Part Three. Politics
- Overall political orientation, beliefs, and values in a nutshell
- Change and continuity in political beliefs over time
- Political practices (e.g., voting, campaigning, rallies, contributions)
- An important life-story scene connected to politics in some way
- Relation between religious faith and politics
- 2004 U.S. Presidential election
- Whom did you vote for? Why?
- Did religious faith affect the choice?
- Why might Christians vote for the other candidate?
- Positive contributions to society
- Other

Generativity is defined, following Erikson, as adults' concern for and commitment to promoting the well-being of future generations. Failures in generativity are assumed to result in feelings of stagnation, and self-preoccupation, while successful generativity is seen as sign of maturity in midlife which promotes psychological health. When is generativity successful? Generativity, operationalized as quantitative measure, with the Loyola Generativity Scale, (LGS), (McAdams & de St. Aubin, 1992) is reported as positively correlated to indicators of familial and social engagement, including religious activities. The "redemptive self" is then introduced as an American life story associated with generativity, redemption is defined as "the deliverance from suffering to an enhanced status or state" (McAdams & Albaugh, 2008a, 265).

The themes organized around it are described as: 1) the protagonist's enjoying a special advantage or blessing in childhood, or some sort of calling, 2) awareness of the suffering of others, 3) establishing strong and clear moral values, often associated with religion, by the time one has reached adolescence, that is, moral steadfastness, and 4) the theme of redemption, which means the experience of overcoming hardship leading to a positive outcome, 5) negotiating power versus love, and 6) prosocial goals. Thus, the redemptive self is a life-narrative form that is well designed to support a generative life.

That there are dark sides of the redemptive self is conceded: Redemptive stories can come across as naïve, arrogant, or self-righteous, complying with an American ideal of individualism. They may neglect the meaning of tragedy in human life.

3.3 *The Story of a Conservative Evangelical and Former Catholic*

Under the headline "redemption and the conflicted life—a conservative Evangelical story" we learn the story of Constance, who is 35 years old at the time of the interview, a mother of two who works part-time as an assistant to a pastor for an evangelical, nondenominational Christian congregation, and for the church she and her family attend, her husband having left a business career to attend a Christian seminary. She has left the Catholic faith of her childhood and together with her husband and children, she is leading a dedicated Christian evangelical life. Her trajectory might be understood as oppositional exit if it involved turning toward a more oppositional religious organization, or, if the new community corresponded to the former in terms of integration in larger society, as religious switching.[10] To decide this, it would be necessary

10 In the study on deconversion we have defined oppositional exit as adopting a different belief system of, or engaging in different ritual praxis in, or affiliation with, a higher-tension, more oppositional religious organization, which could mean e.g. conversion into

to know the status of the respective communities relative to its social context, however, we do not know integrated the Catholic church and the Evangelical congregation are regarded in the part of the US where Constance lives.

How important her faith is to her becomes clear in her response to the interviewer's request to describe how she prays. She "offers a remarkable real-time prayer" (McAdams & Albaugh, 2008a, 267–268) in which she addresses as well as defines the situation: "Father God I thank you that you have called me to this place to meet Michelle (the interviewer). And I don't know what this study is all about and in your economy and in your kingdom, Lord. But there's a reason why you called me to participate in this, and l just pray Lord that you would give us wisdom and discernment. I pray for the people who are doing the study, that you would show them how they are to use this data, that ultimately jt might help people and it might grow and stretch them in their understanding and their knowledge of you and what you plan to do in their lives, and in the lives of those who you love and are called according to your purpose".

With this opening, which, from an analytic perspective can be interpreted as enactment, a presumably unconscious scenic structuring of relationships (cf. Jacobs, 1986), Constance does more than answer the request of the researcher. She makes it clear that in this encounter of science and religion religion comes first by including the researcher who is present as well as the larger project involved in her religious ritual. While she in what she says, welcomes both in her religious world, she also submits herself, the interviewer, and the scientific project to God's higher power. Thus, she is defining the situation as one in which the final authority, regarding the value of the study she is participating in, is with God. Then, she is willing to discuss her faith, which gives her and her family stability: It helps her to resolve conflict, she can forgive her father for having had an affair, and the conflicted abortion-story from her own biography is provided with a redemptive turn. That Constance supports pro-life politics raises the question if she perhaps responds to the need to set something right in the life of others that went wrong in hers, according to her religious standards, which she passes on—which, ironically, may in consequence meet concerns, but also enhance conflict for pregnant teenagers.

That she suspects more liberal agencies to lie to young girls, means at least, that she is still very involved in her own experience, at worst that she is splitting, using the defense of dividing the world into the good, pro-life and

a fundamentalist or new religious group, and religious switching as switching to a religious organization with a similar system of beliefs and rituals and with no difference in terms of integration (Streib, Hood, Keller, Csöff & Silver 2009, 26).

believing, and the bad and non-religious which she can either fight or convert. Thus, her intended generativity may interfere with the next generations' chance for identity development, if we want to stay with Erikson's model. The seamy side of her way of being generative may involve passing on conflict not resolved in her life to the next generation.

The authors contextualize the story within additional findings, drawing on psychoanalytical vocabulary: "The characters in the life stories of evangelicals are often strong-willed people whose lives are subjected to powerful forces for both good and evil. The potential for conflict is ever present. In simple Freudian terms, id impulses do regular battle with a religious superego" (McAdams & Albaugh, 2008a, 273).

3.4 *A Liberal Protestant Voice*

"Redemption and the empty life" covers the story of 44 year old Sally, registered nurse, married to a corporate lawyer. She seems somewhat reluctant to talk about her religion, reverting to the term "spirituality". However, she insists on "dragging the two daughters to church", to "give them something to reject, if nothing else" (McAdams & Albaugh, 2008a, 275). Sally also is concerned about the next generation, and drawing on her own experience: She wants to give her children what she missed in her childhood, e.g. protection from bullying and encouragement to take physical risks. She and her husband express generativity by guiding youth camps and teaching Sunday school. Sally's generativity, involving travelling to impoverished countries, gives her life meaning and purpose. The seamy side of her way of being generative might be that she is filling a void in her rather affluent life with adventurous charities. Thus, both interviewees demonstrate generativity, however, in different ways, in different religious contexts, and with different potential side effects.

Sally's religion is characterized as much more inclusive, her God seems less strict and powerful than Constance's—displaying less strict father morality and more nurturant care-giver characteristics. The authors interpret this difference in terms of differences between ideological life scripts, that is, normativism and humanism, or conservative and liberal value systems. Generativity implies passing on values and ideologies. From a psychoanalytic perspective they might have invoked Winnicott or Rizzuto and speculated about what Constance and Sally took in from their relationships to their parents and how their experiences shaped their images of God. From an attachment-informed perspective we might wonder, what of their religiosity corresponds to that of their parents and where they look for compensation?

MacAdams and Albaugh (2008b) have, in one further publication, focussed on respondents' imaginations of a world without God: They found that politically conservative Christians (scoring high on right-wing authoritarianism) tended to imagine a life deficient in impulse control, wherein unrestrained sexual and aggressive urges, addictive behaviors, and human selfishness undermined the social good. By contrast, politically liberal Christians (scoring low on right-wing authoritarianism) imagined an empty and barren world, devoid of the emotional intensity that makes life worth living. In accord with theoretical writings regarding normative and humanistic ideologies, the findings suggest that, at least among American Christians, political conservatism may entail a fear of, or strong sensitivity to, the prospects of conflict and chaos, whereas political liberalism may entail an equally strong fear of, or sensitivity to, emptiness. From a contemporary and inclusive psychoanalytic perspective, which uses different psychoanalytic psychologies as heuristics (see below) conservatives may, as the authors indicate in the case studies discussed, be concerned with Id-Super-Ego conflicts, while liberals may be searching for good objects.

3.5 *Different Ways of Leaving Jehova's Witnesses: Franz (Germany) and Tom (US)*

Drawing, again, on research from the deconversion study, I offer a comparison of the religious lives of two men, both former Jehova's witnesses, in two different countries. Here, I summarize findings reported in an earlier publication (Keller, Klein, Hood & Streib, 2013) which reported a comparison including quantitative data, structural analyses of religious styles, and interview interpretation. We interviewed, when conducting the deconversion study, deconverts as well as members of a wide variety of religious groups. There are Jehova's witnesses in the US and in Germany, however, being a witness or deconverting, may involve different experiences here compared to there.

Both men were in their fifties when interviewed, both had converted in their twenties and left Jehova's Witnesses after a membership of three decades, and upon conflict with authorities. Both men's biographies are characterized by a troubled childhood with absent fathers and emotionally non-available mothers, and by the experience of war. Franz, in Germany, had lost his older siblings and his father in the Second World War. Tom, in the United States, had after a childhood characterized by neglect, served in the Vietnam War. Both established themselves in their lives, had relationships, neither have children. In the four-options forced-choice format of the binary religious-spiritual of our questionnaire, both claimed to be more spiritual than religious. However, their deconversions follow different trajectories: Franz has been identified as a type of deconvert who, upon leaving, feels "debarred from Paradise," while Tom has been associated to the type of deconvert who is on a "life long quest" or making "late revisions" (cf. Streib et al., 2009).

Comparing Franz' and Tom's individual quantitative profiles with those of current members of oppositional and accommodating religious organizations in Germany reveals: Franz scores significantly lower on emotional stability (reverse scored neuroticism) and extraversion from the Big Five, and comparable to current members on openness, agreeableness and conscientiousness. His scores on all the subscales of Carol Ryff's (Ryff, 1989) instrument of eudaimonic well-being are also significantly lower than those of current members. His scores on the religious fundamentalism scale are lower than the mean for in-tradition members, but higher when compared to other deconverts; and his scores on right-wing authoritarianism are even higher than for current in-tradition members. This may imply that for him deconversion, at least at the time of the interview, involved a loss rather than a gain.

For Tom the comparison with current members looks different: His scores on openness are higher than those of current members and so are his scores on eudaimonic well-being, in particular, on autonomy and personal growth, which may imply that his deconversion brought more gains than losses. His scores on fundamentalism and right-wing authoritarianism are not very different from those of current members. This corresponds to his fundamentalist religious attitude, which was apparent in the interviews, together with his open and reflective stance.

3.6 *Deconversion Narratives and Trajectories*

Here is some biographical background of the deconversion trajectories. Franz, who grew up in a protestant family, however, refused confirmation:

> As is right and proper, I was supposed to go to confirmation classes and be confirmed. Then I have talked to this person there and asked questions about the war and how the Church's position is to these issues; and at that time I learned that the soldiers are [...?]; they went to war with "God with us" and with "Hurra," and I was completely disgusted. And he did not give me a sufficient answer to that, and my reaction was then, "Well, then I will not be confirmed."

With his questions Franz feels also left alone by his mother and his stepfather. Consequentially, his story of his first encounter with Jehova's witnesses is about the "answers" they provided to his big questions which were left open by parents and pastor. When explaining his conversion, he refers to his seeking for orientation, longing for a father:

> How much would I have wished, as a boy, [...] someone who takes me by the hand. And explains to me what life is about. Actually, this, this was what I always, still as a young person, ahm, was waiting for.

Franz portrays himself as naïve young person who was lured into the ideology of the witnesses. This account stands in a certain tension to other parts of his narrative, which describe that he later held positions of teaching and pastoral care in the JW community:

> My career the, with the witnesses, I was, first, as they say, ministerial servant or deacon. Then, two or three years later, elder. Then I did several things, but almost everything there, starting with steward, treasurer, ah, servant, and I have directed the school for, ahm, long time—the study of the watchtower.

Franz was well-integrated when conflict arose with a visiting elder who criticized his activities. When, again, his questions and objections, although based on Bible studies, were not answered and authorities did not live up to moral expectations, when there was no response to his appeals to solve the conflict, he stepped back from his responsibilities and finally left. He regrets that, due to JW expectations that Armageddon would be in 1975, he and his wife did not have children. He also regrets to have discontinued seeing his relatives, due to the command of the witnesses. Being disfellowshipped after decades with the witnesses only, he and his wife feel isolated. Franz is reluctant to join a religious group ever again, while keeping his faith. Therefore we categorized his deconversion as privatizing exit.

Tom from the United States also tells a story of a troubled childhood. His mother led an instable life, had children of different fathers, some of them were given up for adoption. Tom's narrative is about growing up around emotionally unavailable and unpredictable caretakers. Later Tom served in the Vietnam War and, upon his return, worked in the IT-sector. He cultivated a critical view on Christianity, which he saw as corrupted, observed self-proclaimed Christians who were involved in sinful acts. This led him to accept the Jehovah's Witnesses' invitation to intensive Bible study and finally affiliate with the JW. The reason he gives for his conversion is that, upon having grown up in an "emotional vacuum" he was "looking for structure". In his deconversion narrative he shows appreciation of what he gained:

> And, it provided an excellent uhm, environment in which to really get into the scriptures because it's a fundamentalist religion.

Tom also tells in the interview that he underwent a process of change:

> Bible is the bottom line. Uhm … I gradually got to the point though, where that was no longer working for me.

He explains what he came to perceive as shortcomings in the JW community:

> And so they're missing spirit, they're missing relationships, and I was hungry for that more and more and more … and just not finding it there. Went to all the different elders looking for answers, and uhm, as I got more and more frustrated uhm … I settled down and I read through the Bible three times in the course of four years.

In these independent Bible studies he discovers that God was, in the New Testament, referred to as father. This speaks to his interest in relationship. When the elders cannot share his views conflict arises, culminating in his being disfellowshipped.

> And, unlike most who are disfellowshipped, who feel all of a sudden you know, cast out of the life boat, for me it was a sense of relief.

Tom does not seem to feel as a victim nor does he report regrets. He has moved on to a more liberal denomination which he believes filled the void left by the Jehovah's Witness community. We identified Tom's deconversion trajectory as an integrating exit.

3.7 *Transformation as Change in Religious Style or Structural Deconversion*

A closer view into the faith development interview with Franz, shows a predominantly mythic-literal style. After leaving the Jehovah's Witnesses, Franz continues to take the guidelines for a Christian life literally from the Bible. With reference to Hood, Hill and Williamson (2005), this can be interpreted as fundamentalist, as an intratextual understanding. His deconversion seems to have been more an issue of rejecting specific prescriptions (or rather their interpretation by the church authorities), than an issue of applying a new level of reasoning about religious matters. In his faith development interview, Franz states that he would rely on the commandments of the Bible if he had to make important decisions, and only secondary ask whether the decision is reasonable and feasible:

> Uh, well, I'll think about this. A-firstly, well, in accordance with, uh ... the Biblical commands or principles, not commands, we don't have those anymore, okay with the Biblical principles, uh, then reason, this decision, is it reasonable, is it advisable to do something like that. This is the way I would. And then the do-ability of it.

Franz does not show many signs of a change of religious style. His adherence to a mythic-literal form of faith, his reproach against the witnesses, whom he now sees as misrepresenting the sacred texts, and his image of God as a powerful parental (father) figure, whose commands he has to obey in order to be accepted, point to what Streib has defined as an instrumental-reciprocal religious style. Tom's faith development interview was evaluated as indicating the development of individuative-reflective Faith. Tom himself comments on his development:

> Uhm, just in the past few months have I finally moved over the line between teenager and adult.

Thus, we have some evidence of a structural deconversion. In Tom's faith development interview, scores range from Stage Three to Stage Five. His scores thus span a range of two stages. For the case of fundamentalist religiosity, heterodyning of styles has been introduced, together with the corollary, that "the mutuality or the individuative reflectiveness resists complete submission and surrender to the fundamentalist demand" and eventually this leads to the perception of contradictions (Streib, 2001, 154). This seems to apply to Tom, who throughout his faith development interview shows a reflective and explicit way of dealing with issues of truth and interpretation of the Bible, and regarding his own past. Here, he is reasoning about his difficulties to see God as father:

> Well, with both my fathers, they're significant by virtue of having been just about null. And so not willful neglect but neglect, the emptiness none the less. [I.: Right.] That's significant because it leaves me with an emptiness, left me with a real difficulty as seeing God as my father. [I.: Mhm.] because my awareness of what a father is a presence that does nothing. [I.: Mhm.] And ... shifting that relative to a father who is out of sight and works indirectly—[I.: Right.] has been a challenge.

To illustrate the most advanced style present, we quote from Tom's response to the question how Tom would generally go about decision-making, which has been scored Stage Five, conjunctive faith:

> Prayer, prayer and meditation and somewhere in the course it will come to me. [I.: How ... how or when did you sort of come to that model of decision making?] (long pause for thinking) [...] I grew up uhm ... extremely left brained. Personal decisions, personal work it out, figure out the logic of it, and come to the conclusions. And parallel with all of that was an intense fear of faith because my understanding of faith was blind faith. [I.: Mhm.] What I saw in Hebrews 11:1 is that we need foundation for our faith. We need evidence. [I.: Mhm.] and as I came to understand that I began to open up to something more than just what I could see, measure, analyze, etc. [I.: Mhm.] and ... growing accustomed to that, allowing myself to go in that direction has been a very long process. [I.: Mhm.] Uhm ... but I understood—[...] that my heart was totally shut down, but heart is what I needed in order to be able to do all this stuff. [I.: Right.] And I didn't have a clue, how do I get the heart to open up the heart? [I.: Yeah.] But I just decided somehow I just got to have it. The scriptures say, „ask and ye shall receive" that's what I am going to do. [...]—and so it took years before that process speeded up enough and there had been enough healing and enough faith to allow myself to heal more rapidly. [...] So, to answer your question of how and where—[I.: Yeah.] it's just been a very gradual process.

Here, Tom describes how he struggled to move toward a new religious orientation, involving, "the heart", or basic trust in the terms of Rizzuto's (Eriksonian) language, and in line with Streib's description of the dialogical style.

3.8 *Psychodynamic Perspectives*

According to the classical assumption we can frame transformation as cancellation of a "crooked cure" (Freud, 1921, 142). Tom and Franz corrected, by deconverting, the decisions of the young men, who, instead of facing the harsh realities of their respective upbringings, were seeking the consolation of a religious community which provided answers (Franz) and structure (Tom). Deconversion resulted, when this proved illusionary (Franz) or at least one-sided (Tom). An Ego-psychology perspective would emphasize that both men in their respective troubled childhoods had insufficient possibilities to acquire reality testing, adaptive skills, and defenses. Their faith, giving answers and structure, served as compensation of an inner defense against drive, and supported their adaptation to the outside world (Hartmann, 1958). Transformation would then refer to pervasive change in ego-functioning. This might be inferred from Tom's self-reflective and perceptive review of his development, as well as from his statement, that he felt relief upon leaving. For Franz, who feels devastated upon leaving this seems to be a challenge. Self-psychology might ask if lack of early mirroring and empathy lead to difficulties in the formation of a self that is experienced as strong, vital, and cohesive. This may have lead Franz to look for support in form of a religious community with a reliable doctrine offered by father figures. Still vulnerable to disappointments after deconversion, he finds fault with them, not with his expectations. However, in the exit group he joined, he may find empathy and mirroring when sharing his experience. Tom, who started to look for structure to find himself turning to a new search for "the heart", shows self-awareness, when he realizes that this change of direction—transformation—involves his biography and his decisions. An object relations view might focus on early relationship experience condensed in object representations. The conflicts with the elders might be read as repetitions of early drama: Again the father figures showed lack of interest and understanding. Transformation can be inferred from change in God representations, as indicated by Tom's turn to fatherly aspects. On a more sophisticated level, it would involve reflection and self-reflection, tying earlier to current experiences and perspectives, resulting in acknowledgment of one's own and others limitations—as we see in Tom's, less so in Franz' interview data: Tom shows awareness of his difficulties around relationships to others and to God. Franz hardly articulates the deep disappointment by earlier and later relationships that he feels, arguing rather along standards of right and wrong (see tables 1.1, 4.1).

With taking Mitchell's model we can discern how the different modes of interaction structure the religious trajectories:

Franz' religious search seems mainly concerned with the regulation of interactions, mode 1—reciprocal influence. He is also thinking about others with whom he can get together, striving to follow Jesus' words and build a congregation. He is affiliated with a support-group of other ex-witnesses, with whom he can share feelings and experiences (mode 2, affective permeability), positioning himself in the group and his experience against theirs (mode 3, self-other configurations), starting to reflect his story which might eventually open up functioning on mode 4, intersubjectivity—and thus support transformation.

The heterodyning we see in Tom's profile of aspects might be constructed as the joint and dominant presence of mode 1 (nonreflective behavior, reciprocal influence) and 3 (self-other configurations)—indicating, according to his narrative, longstanding concern with these particular modes and challenges toward integration with the other modes of interaction. Relations with others might still be an issue for Tom. He describes his relationship with God as major concern, when asked what he would like to change about himself: "That's an ongoing process. Uhm ... the measure of intimacy that I have with God. That relationship…". He is looking for intimacy (mode 2, shared affective experience), which has not played a major role in his life so far, implying, that transformation involves change there, and that Tom's self-reflective stance allows him to make this statement.

3.9 *Mentalization and Epistemic Trust / Distrust*

Here, the clinical and typological operationalization of the mentalization approach is used for interpretation. From an attachment-informed perspective, both men may have been looking for something compensating for their insecure early relationships.

In his interview Franz looks back on how he was lured into the community of the JW. However, his reconstruction may also point to the readiness of the young man for taking their offers as "ostensive cues", which gave him the impression that he was seen with his questions and concerns, and that he was offered valuable knowledge on how the world works (Fonagy et al., 2017, 2). This may have inspired, what in hindsight looks like epistemic credulity, "triggered by a hyperactive or unmoored social imagination generating a personal narrative that is so diffuse that the individual concerned is unable to judge whether another person's perception of them is accurate" (Fonagy, Luyten, Allison & Campbell, 2019, 4).

> First, I have well, learned, learned many new things. Scripture, which then again is related to what (clearing his throat) watchtower says. Got some things straight, right? What actually leads us as human beings to salvation, all these precautions ahm, and have also that Christ came as our saviour. No matter what else was written. Was consolidating myself, only, then came, that, what the watchtower society teaches, that this contradicts the bible. But you can't realize that so soon. Not if you are a witness, for an active witness, who is visiting the congregation, it is impossible to look through that.

It seems that in Franz' view religious literature should correspond to scripture and life practice should be in accordance with both. Sacred text is understood as referring to reality. There is no space for different views or interpretations, nor other minds suggesting different readings. What is in the sacred text corresponds to sacred reality, a reality not to be played with. Other perspectives are perceived as threat to reality per se because there has to be one truth—and are consequently discounted as wrong.

This might be read as indications of the "equivalence mode" in terms of mentalization (Fonagy & Target, 2007). Franz does not show much self-reflection.

His own inner states seem opaque to him. The serious depressive states he experienced felt to him like a fatigue which he did not understand, nor could he make sense of the mood swings which he experienced throughout his life. The exit group, which he joined upon deconversion may provide a secure base encouraging him to explore his (and others') inner worlds more deeply, to gain realistic epistemic trust, and to move toward transformation understood as pervasive change of his relating toward himself as well as toward the transcendent.

Tom claims that his life has been without "real connections" to other persons until his early twenties. He reflects on his life, stating, that the lack of attachment to father figures is a challenge in his relationship to God. He may have used his time with Jehova's witnesses not only to gain "structure", but also to gain trust—in his own abilities to understand the bible and to relate to what he learned. He shows awareness of his own and others' inner states, of process, when he discusses relationships and changes in his relationships. This stands in tension to the area of faith, where he is strictly adhering to his Christian faith in a rather fundamentalist style. Asked how religious conflicts can be resolved, he states:

> with a lot of prayer and grace. If they can be resolved at all. A lot of forgiveness ... In order to resolve religious differences there needs to be on the part of both parties, a desire to serve Christ. And a faith in his willingness and ability to be the light and then ... a lot of prayer as I mentioned and an appreciation that uhm, sometimes because of coming from different backgrounds it may take a lot of work to resolve those differences, but there has to be flexibility. And humility that allows one to recognize 'I haven't got all the answers.'

Notwithstanding the humility offered, everything is to be brought under the authority of Christ.

The comparisons offered can be called idiothetic: They are based on autobiographical narratives, on reviews of lives in specific circumstances, compared by drawing on "principles" taken from psychoanalytic literature, faith development theory, and for the German-American comparison, on psychometrics / scales.

4 Religion and Faith "in Treatment"

4.1 *Clinical Aspects*

For a discussion of clinical aspects I want to give an overview on some psychoanalysts who discuss working with religious issues or problems in psychotherapeutic treatment. Again, this is a spotlight, not a comprehensive picture. Table 4.1 presents again different analytical orientations toward religion, here with references of examples of clinical applications.

TABLE 4.1 Analytical orientations and attitudes toward religion

Analytical orientation	**Reference to religion**	**Recognition, Revision, and** ***religious interventions***
Drive theory	God as parental figure, protection against breakthrough of drive	I. Ostov 2007
Ego psychology	Faith as support / surrogate for ego-functions	*W. W. Meissner 2001*
Self-psychology	Selfobject—function vs "false self"	P. Holliman 2002
Object relations theories	God representation, transitional space	A.-M. Rizzuto 1979
Intersubjectivity / Relational perspective / Mentalization	Religious experience, anchored in relationality reflected	*M. T. Hoffman 2011* J. W. Jones 1996 R. L. Sorenson 2004 Schaap-Jonker and Corveleyn 2014, Keller and Streib 2013

Engaging with the "Junktim", the inseparable bond between cure and research (Freud, 1927b, 255), I present a case "in treatment", in which religiosity structured the patient's experience considerably, although he had adopted a critical perspective toward his Catholic upbringing. I will report on an analysis with a middle aged male patient, first seen in short term psychodynamic therapy, which was then expanded to a psychoanalysis with 2–3 sessions per week and in the classical setting.

4.2 *Introducing the Patient*

The patient was a man in his forties, with an academic education, working in a technological profession, divorced, a daughter. He came to therapy in acute crisis, which arose when living with a woman, whom he had, together with her adolescent children, allowed to live with him in his small apartment. Under these conditions the new relationship took a dramatic turn. The woman he had adored and wanted to rescue from her financial difficulties mutated, as he perceived it, into a fury who exploited him. There were violent scenes, which made him call the police. Because she refused to leave the apartment, he moved out and took a lawyer.

He was suffering from moderate depression, harmful use of tobacco, because he had started smoking again. Treatment started as short term psychodynamic therapy. When, after successful crisis intervention, the compulsive organization of his personality became apparent, psychoanalysis was planned (see also Table 4.2).

Mr. M. has grown up in rural poverty in eastern Europe, where the family lived on a farm. The family was Catholic, and his mother cared for a strict religious upbringing of the children, adhering to a rigid form of faith herself. Both parents were refugees who had to leave their country, when borders were redrawn after World War II in this part of Europe, and they found themselves declared "foreign", probably both were traumatized. While the mother looked to the Catholic church for stability and comfort, the father, who could barely provide for the family on the little farm, used alcohol to balance his moods. The patient was an intelligent child who liked school, was interested in acquiring knowledge, and achieved considerable success, when he, because of his excellent performance, was admitted to Gymnasium.[11] As schoolkid he had his first jobs, for example, delivering mail, to cover the costs for his drivers' license. He left home to study mechanical engineering in the big city hundreds of kilometers away. He financed his studies with jobs and scholarships, however did not finish them, when he decided to not return home from travelling to the UK but to stay there with his girlfriend and later wife. He worked there as carpenter on construction sites, until both decided to go to Germany. There he acquired after a tough start his degree as business engineer, and is, at the time of the beginning of treatment, working in an engineering company.

I draw on the report to the reviewer which is part of the formal application for psychoanalysis in the German health system:[12] The patient, who could gain

11 This is a secondary school leading to an A-level exam ('Abitur'), which allows to apply at universities.

12 In the German health system the therapist writes an anonymized "report to the reviewer" (Bericht an den Gutachter) which, for psychoanalysis, consists of relevant sociodemographic data, symptoms presented and mental state, including transference-countertransference, somatic status (analysts with a psychological university degree send their patients to a medical doctor to get a statement on their status), biographical data, anamnesis, psychodynamics (inner conflicts and what activated them), diagnosis, treatment plan and prognosis. This report goes, with the patient's application, to a reviewer, who reports to the health insurance company of the patient. The insurance companies follow the recommendation of the reviewers when deciding on funding treatment.

TABLE 4.2 Mr. M.'s diagnosis structured according to the different psychoanalytical psychologies

Analytical orientation	Asssessment of Mr. M.
Drive theory	Rigid superego
Ego psychology	Turn against his own person, denial, reaction formation, idealization, intellectualization and isolation of affect
Self-psychology	False self, religious commandments structure affect
Object relations theories	Ambivalent inner objects
Intersubjectivity / relational	Self-sufficient, useful to others, following rules
perspective / Mentalization	Psychic equivalence

enough stability to settle his threatened housing and working situation, sees himself on one side as someone who has to make an effort, to take control, and to be as self-sufficient as possible in order to meet the ups and downs of life. On the other side he starts to feel his tremendous longing for being allowed to let go, to be held, and for relationship, which he so far lived by caring for others, always ready to feel guilty for his own needs.

The symptoms presented were presumably caused by the failure of the new romantic attachment relationship on which the patients had put high hopes. The failure of this attempt at finding attachment or a self-object may be read as repetition of an early attachment trauma. The patient's attempt to save a woman he barely knew, together with her children, from financial difficulties, refers to an unconscious mission: He set out to save his mother, who had been disappointed by the father, while, at the same time, unconsciously being afraid to also fail—like his father.

Between a demanding and complaining mother and a father who neglected the family, the patient had lived between being flooded by affect and feeling ignored. He had learned early to look after himself and be useful to others to keep otherwise not very supportive relationships. Aggressive affects were inhibited and are a considerable inner threat for him. Not used to explore inner experiences and impressions he is after the recent crisis weighed down by depressive affects which are unfamiliar to him and cause, in addition, anxiety (see also Table 4.3).

There was not much space in his life so far for the exploration of his personal feelings and inner states. It seems that, above all, religious Catholic, commandments structured his emotions. Consequently, therapy focused on working with him toward a less harsh Super-Ego, toward establishing ego functions instead of reliance on commandments, and on the perception and differentiation of his inner states, his affects and emotions. In the course of therapy he acquired more differentiated representations of his relationships and of his interactions with others.

TABLE 4.3 General approaches to the treatment of Mr. M. according to psychoanalytic perspectives

Analytical orientation	Mr. M. in treatment
Drive theory	Milder superego
Ego psychology	Stabilization of ego functions
Self-psychology	Better affect perception and differentiation
Object relations theories	Differentiated perspective on relationships past and present
Intersubjectivity / relational perspective /	Secure frame, reliable availability, exploration of Emotions
Mentalization	Marked mirroring, questioning

In terms of modes of interaction (Mitchell) on the basic non-reflective level of patterns of interaction a stable frame was established (treatment hours, responsibility for attending session, working relationship). Such a frame allows the exploration of affect and emotion (affective permeability). On the level of self-other configuration the patient explored how he related to others as son, partner, father, etc. Intersubjectivity refers to understanding one's own and others' inner lives. Conflicts with others, conflicts in the therapeutic situation and pertaining affects and emotions were processed, symbolized, and could thus be shared and negotiated.

For example: When the patient had developed enough trust by attending regularly and relying on the therapist to be there to listen to him, he could share his rage at his former partner, found relieve in sharing phantasies of retaliation, while he could restrain himself in reality. This means that he vented his anger in phantasies during the sessions and could refrain from damaging her car. Later, he was able to reflect on this dramatic episode of his life, which had started with his wish to rescue her like a good man, a "gentleman" and different from his father who drank and neglected the family. He could share his disappointment and explore how he related to women, in reporting on his encounters with women and in negotiating the relationship to his female analyst.

4.3 *Religious Development and Current Attitudes*

Religion for him was related to rules and laws. From the perspective of the religious styles, we might draw on different styles to describe him: On the level of reciprocal instrumental faith, Mr. M.'s faith seemed to show orientation toward rules and punishment, but also longing for protection and security. He showed individuative reflection, when he discussed his Catholic faith as a system from which he keeps a critical distance. There was room for development: he discussed perhaps to go to church again in a distant future, however, seeing this, similar to therapy, as an option to find relief from the challenges of everyday life, thus more oriented toward his personal experience than toward specific content or doctrine.

He saw himself as striving to keep the ten commandments. However, he observed that many people do not obey those. Perhaps it would be better to also be immoral, a pig? However, he appreciated his Catholic upbringing as strict and keeping him grounded. It helped him to become a decent guy. There was conflict with his mother who objected to his divorce. Would he live in sin if he took up a new relationship again? When his father died, he did not go to communion, did not wish to confess. He stated that he did not trust priests, that he considered them as hypocrites, greedy, and corrupt. His religious attitudes structured his moral convictions, notwithstanding his criticisms. In Rizzuto's terms, he may have been among "those wondering whether or not to believe in a God they are not sure exists" (Rizzuto, 1979, 91).

4.4 *From the Sessions: Interventions*

Mr. M. reports a dream of his deceased father. He woke up with the impression that his father is angry with him. I ask him: What would you want? He answers: That father comes closer and that he is more friendly. I point out: It is your dream. You could imagine that your dream is similar to a movie, which you have directed. His first response is relief: My father is not angry with me. Then there is uncertainty: It is hard to admit that everything ends with death. He shares thoughts on mortality, remembers his philosophy class, and states that it would be childish to invent concrete images of an afterlife.

I asked him: Do you believe in God? He answered: "I think I do, in spite of the mathematics I have studied so long. This is on the one hand, irrational, on the other, it would be nice." This resonates with Bartlett's observation of the fluidity of religion as belief (Bartlett, 1950, p17) as well as with Will's comment on the necessity to attend to one's belief and to one's unbelief in a reflexive way (Will, 2014b, 164).

TABLE 4.4 Analytical approaches to work with Mr. M.'s religiosity

Analytical orientation	Mr. M.'s religiosity
Drive theory	Protection and inhibition by religious commandments
Ego psychology	Thoughts and feelings toward his religious experiences: longings and criticisms
Self-psychology	Gentleman—and what else?
Object relations theories	God as father figure: strict, just
Intersubjectivity / relational perspective / Mentalization	Could he trust God—and his own critical thinking?

When he left treatment, he stated: "I have learned to talk about my soul in German". He has gained more awareness of his inner processes, learned how to symbolize what he perceives, and, moreover, trust in his ability to handle conflicting emotions.

4.5 *On Putting Experience into Words: Bion and Transformation in "O"*

When Mr. M. came to treatment he did not have much experience with perceiving and handling inner experience. Here, a perspective is helpful, which can be categorized as belonging to object relations theory, however, offers a specific approach for working with ineffable inner states, with basic experiences, which can occur in psychosis, in science, and in religion, and for which there are no words yet. The task in therapy is then, to "contain", to hold the inchoate experience of the patient and to help them develop for what Wilfred Bion found the expression "alpha function", to support them to move toward symbolizing their experience.

Alpha function can break down under stress or in psychosis: "When alpha-function is attacked, psychotics lose the ability to discern that there is anything other than beta-elements—anything other than psychic reality." (Merkur, 2010, 240). By "reverie", a relaxed as well as attentive openness toward the patient, the analyst is with the patient in a way that supports the transformation of psychic reality into experience. Merkur (2010, 245) summarizes: "The goal of the analyst's meditation was the psychoanalytic process; it was simultaneously a mystical union." He also notes: "Bion opened psychoanalytic discourse to an explicit and open exploration of the mystical, apparently by offering what he regarded as a 'geocentric language'" (Merkur, 2010, 250). Merkur here refers to Bion drawing on the usage of everyday language, which works for us, although it contradicts scientifically proven facts: "Let's get up tomorrow at sunrise" functions for communication and planning, although semantically it belongs to a worldview no longer valid. On the other hand, he would not want to abolish heliocentric astronomy. To me, he seems to be aware of different ways of knowing.

Bion conceptualized the very procedures of clinical psychoanalysis as a mystical practice. The analyst serves implicitly as the analysand's spiritual director. Both analyst and analysand meditate. When therapy is successful, both achieve "transformations of O," which was Bion's term for mystical reversions from the perceptible many to the intelligible forms of the unknowable godhead (Merkur, 2010, 228).

Eigen, who also portrayed Bion as psychoanalytic mystic, states in his chapter "Musings on O": "Bion notes the surprising degree of agreement by mystics expressing their meeting with ultimate reality." And later on the same page 83 he compiles what Bion says on religion: "If religion is an illusion (Freud, 1927a) Bion (1992) called it a *basic* illusion (p.374), a term that recalls his "basic assumptions" in groups (1961). 'Any particular religion changes with the prevalent fashion, but the fundamental thing, religion itself, does not' (1992, 374). Bion (1992) notes that religion—the fundamental thing—is a powerful force, although we do not know exactly what this powerful force is. In fact, he calls it a very powerful force (p. 374) and recalls the Death pit at Ur and the deaths of 900 followers of Jim Jones in Guayana in 1978. To think we know what this force is is to prematurely trivialize it. It will not stop exerting itself on account of our trivializations." I suggest to see Bion's conception of religion as fundamental thing as resonating with mysticism understood as personally experienced and indidualized form of religiosity, and as including a specific context of discovery: Unconscious experience (Eigen, 1998, 83).

4.6 *Boundary Issues: Psychoanalysis, Psychotherapy, Religion and World Views*

Eigen puts forward an inclusive perspective, when he states in the introduction to his book on the "Psychoanalytic mystic": "For me, there are moments when psychoanalysis is a form of prayer. There is, too, a meditative dimension in psychoanalytic work. Psychoanalytical-mystical openness to the unknown overlap. Analytic workers, not religious in the literal sense, may be touched by intimations of something sacred in the work" (Eigen, 1998). There is continuing discussion on this issue and as lowest common denominators analytical concepts like abstinence or neutrality can be invoked.

This means that in each treatment it has to be carefully weighed what is helpful to give the patient their space to explore their feelings, relationships, and commitments, including their religiosity, between harsh rejection of what may be deemed sacred, and violating boundaries. There are no easy general answers to questions like: Should a therapist reveal their religious identification? Say a prayer with the patient? Visit a sacred place with the patient? Sorry, but it is complex and it depends, and it is, like with other tender issues, important to provide space for process and reflection, if necessary, with the support of inter- or supervision.

5 Conclusions: The Value of Complementary Perspectives

I have suggested to combine the different perspectives of psychometrics and psychoanalysis for more depth of focus in the psychology of religion. My review has been necessarily selective and limited according to my training, skills, and interests. There is more to discover and to discuss on the way toward a scientifically versed psychoanalytic psychology of religion and a psychoanalytically versed academic psychology of religion. For example, from psychoanalytic psychology of religion, the work of C. G. Jung and J. Lacan deserves attention, and for psychoanalysts further inspection of current qualitative and quantitative methods of capturing aspects of religious experience might be inspiring.

Now I want to get back to the guiding metaphor of this text and revisit, in this concluding section, the complementary perspectives of nomothetic and idiothetic research and of local or indigenous and global or general concepts and methods. I will recommend the cultivation of hybrids, as well as scientific self-reflection, and, finally, line out some future directions.

5.1 *Idiothetic—Nomothetic*

The neologism "idiothetic" was coined by Lamiell. He suggests to cultivate "idiothetic" methods to work from single cases toward general and theoretically meaningful results. This resonates with psychoanalytic attention to careful analyses of single cases, which are then used for theorizing. It is a challenge to current psychological mainstream's reliance on "knowledge of the average", which, in Lamiell's view is too often (mis-)taken for "knowledge of the general".

The aim is to create, monitor, and continuously adapt designs, which combine methods and research perspectives in an ongoing process of identifying general insights without losing the foundation of individual experience implying:

- Moving beyond the single case as moving from idiographic to idiothetic.
- Moving beyond average to general, informed by careful study of single cases.
- Methodologically controlled options to take the careful study of the single case as point of departure, to define characteristics, then use those to move beyond the single case, e.g. by further comparisons and elaboration of typologies, to work from idiographic to idiothetic (Lamiell 1981, 2019), and provide a complementary perspective beyond dominant nomothetic versus (less dominant) idiographic strategies.

Luyten and Corveleyn have, in their review of the controversy between attachment versus depth psychology pointed out that the different cultures of natural science versus interpretive science are involved (Luyten & Corveleyn, 2007). Translated to Lamiell's vocabulary, they argue for creative combinations of idiothetic and nomothetic research strategies.

In a similar vein, Fonagy and Campbell recently referred to another founding figure in the social sciences, stating that Weber's ideal type can be read as resonating with ideas of how to do attend to individual experience, when looking for options for meaningful abstractions and generalizations. They contend: "Weber's (1923) concept is helpful not just at the sociological level but also in the consideration of the organization of human cognition. 'An ideal type is formed by the one-sided accentuation of one or more points of view and by the synthesis of a great many diffuse, discrete, more or less present and occasionally absent concrete individual phenomena, which are arranged according to those one-sidedly emphasized viewpoints into a unified analytical construct'" (Fonagy & Campbell, 2015, 245, note 1).

This corresponds to notions of an idiothetic approach, where the analysis of a single case is used as point of departure for generalizations—and not as mere illustration of correlational or other analyses on group level.

The study of single cases can be seen as a starting point for further enquiry of differences and similarities between individuals, leading to generalizations, and thus, moving from idiographic to idiothetic, complementing nomothetic research based on "objective" measures. An additional argument for the defense of the "novella" is, that case studies allow re-interpretations. It is possible to review and revise what was once told. For an example from psychoanalysis, see Hare-Mustin (1983) on "Dora".

5.2 *Local—Global*

As we focus upon religion in a more and more global perspective, we are reminded that much of the psychology of religion has been focused upon and studied by WEIRD people—the acronym for "Western, educated, industrialized, rich, and democratic" societies (Hood et al., 2018, 505). The study of religion involves acknowledgment of the existence of different religious traditions as different perspectives on human existence. These may resonate in different ways with different psychologies (cf. Abu-Raiya's work on "Western Psychology and Muslim Psychology in Dialogue" (Abu-Raiya, 2014)). As Jensen's recent study on early psychoanalysis shows, different traditions can inspire an emerging psychology in different ways: It was possible for people from very different—western and eastern—cultural and religious surrounds, namely in in Berlin, London and Calcutta, to relate to the then new psychoanalytic project (Jensen 2019).

As the case studies offered demonstrate, religious lives are located in time and place, and what people believe matters in their lives. Psychology of religion may listen to "indigeneous" stories, to stories of different times and places, in which different personal lives in the contexts of different ideologies, wars, economies, legislations, social conditions, etc., are remembered and narrated.

We can, however, only talk about difference when we are able to draw comparisons. This implies that we need dialogue about standards and lines of comparison, on different levels of observation and abstraction. We are, in Bielefeld and Chattanooga, collecting data and experiences, as the Faith Development Interview and the M-scale are used in different translations and in different cultural and religious contexts. This is necessarily based on interreligious and intercultural teamwork and on interdisciplinary dialogue.

5.3 *Scientific Self-Reflections and Minding Others' Faiths*

Lamiell offers, as foundation of his criticisms, a critical historical perspective on the study of human difference and development, looking back on roads not taken, to the disappointment of one of its founding figures, William Stern. Stern was concerned about the loss of the personal in the then new differential psychology and its adoption of correlational methods based on tests and questionnaires. Lamiell also reminds psychology of its roots in philosophy, and attending to the perils of translation, he points out that "Geisteswissenschaften" (sciences of the mind) once have been conceptualized as "Erfahrungswissenschaften" (sciences of experience) and could, nowadays, be more than "humanities" (Lamiell, 2019, 167–168). By reminding psychology of roads not taken, he opens up new vistas to consider.

Controversial discussions also accompanied the changes and revisions that psychoanalysis saw in the many years after Freud. A recent critical review takes up its central traditional myth. Jürgen Kind, German psychoanalyst, notes that Freud reduced the oedipal myth to the son, who murdered his father and had incest with mother, omitting the murderous intentions of both his parents, their conflicted and violent history, and Oedipus' later killing of his own sons.

Kind states that Freud stayed mute on parental transgressions. Thus he extends the discussion of the Oedipus-complex to the generation of parents and grandparents, shifting the crime to filicide. He uses what he diagnoses as remarkable neglect to shed light on corresponding issues in the history of psychoanalysis: Power games and transgressions within psychoanalytic groups and institutions were denied instead of remembered and worked through—as self-reflective usage of psychoanalytic knowledge and skills would suggest (Kind, 2017).

Another psychoanalytic option of self-monitoring is "Konzeptforschung" (Concept research, see Leuzinger-Bohleber & Fischmann, 2006) as explicit research program for monitoring content and usage of basic concepts which are used to structure scientific research and clinical application. A (self-)critical historical perspective and openness toward perspective-taking might support productive interdisciplinary work in the psychology of religion.

Luyten and Corveleyn suggested, in their historically informed review of the attachment versus depth psychology / psychoanalysis discussion in the psychology of religion, that researchers dare leave the secure bases of their convictions (Luyten & Corveleyn, 2007) and engage in perspective-taking. Granqvist's review of his own role as proponent of the conflict may be read as fine example of remembering and working through in the context of scientific debate (Granqvist 2020). This recent discussion raises the debate to the level of critically and self-critically monitoring processes of scientific discussion and, moreover, of attitudes toward different approaches and methods, and of prioritisations of research questions.

5.4 *Some Future Directions*

Methods like the M-scale and the Faith Development Interview, which explore religious experience in its basic elements as well as in its biographical context, have been used in different cultural surrounds and proven to be useful for exploring particularities as well as general characteristics of experience. For future work concepts with the potential to bridge or even integrate different disciplinary perspectives, like mentalization or epistemic trust seem promising. Focussing on the awareness of one's own and others' inner worlds, on when to rely on others' knowledge or when to doubt is, these concepts hold potential for the psychological study of religion and, in particular, pertaining to models of religious development.

Mentalization has been operationalized on the level of modes (typological), as rating scale based on interview evaluation, and, recently, as self-report scale. There are parallels in the study of religious development, where evaluations of the Faith Development Interview can yield individual structural profiles, which are used in case studies which can be organized in typologies. It can also yield frequencies of style assignments, corresponding to an ordinal scale, and, with the Religious Scheme Scale (Streib, Hood & Klein 2010) a nomothetic measure is available.

Thus, there are options for explorations on different methodological levels, of teasing out the strengths and weaknesses of each operationalizations, spanning from idiographic to nomothetic. Mentalization / epistemic trust and Faith Development / religious styles can thus be operationalized in different ways in an interdisciplinary space shared by theories and concepts from developmental psychology, differential psychology, and psychology of religion—all of which are also addressed in psychoanalytic psychology.

The joint perspectives of psychoanalysis and psychometrics might be productively used in the further exploration of Faith Develoment, with mentalization as a bridging concept, allowing to formulate hypotheses drawing on the unconscious. This may show in what is called "fresh speech" in attachment vocabulary in the course of, for example, faith development interviews, and, in a different way, during experiments which elicit responses outside conscious awareness.

The concept of religion as cultural container might be used for theorizing on religion and place, concrete in landscape and geography as well as symbolized in art and poetry. How are traditional religious places experienced? How do people who consider themselves more or less religious, spiritual, or else, respond to such places? Is it true that "someone will forever be surprising a hunger in himself to be more serious" (Larkin)? What kind of personal religion do migrants and refugees bring with them and how do they cultivate it?

Religion has always travelled, it was adopted, assimilated, integrated as part of culture and cultural identity, developed toward "tradition": Christianity, now often named together with "west", has its roots in the middle East. It seems that humans have, again and again, developed a tendency to feel "no longer at ease in the old dispensations" and looked for a different "religion" or for more fulfilling ways to relate to something larger than their everyday lives. Climate change is a growing global concern. How we participate in it and respond to it is studied from an analytical perspective by Orange, who calls for radical (universal) ethics and appeals to our responsibility for what happens elsewhere in the world, but contingent on our habits and life style (Orange, 2017).

And moreover, we have to meet another global challenge: At the time of this writing the Corona Virus has already changed the lives of millions of people worldwide. Politicians appeal to personal responsibility when they ask for radical adjustments to conditions so far unknown and unexplored. The discussions of possible reasons and of coping strategies motivated me to look again to Günther Anders' work. In his later years and having left the US not for Germany, but Vienna in Austria, he wrote about "Die Antiquiertheit des Menschen" (The Obsolescence of Man), presenting three theses: 1. that we as human beings are not up to the perfection of the machines which we can produce, 2. that we can produce more than we can imagine and take responsibility for, and 3. that we believe that we are allowed to do what we can do. He dedicated his work to the memory of his father, mindful of William Stern's hope to be able to vindicate the person by arguing against an impersonal psychology.

The Sterns were rather critical toward psychoanalysis. However, the concern with lack of conscious awareness of our thoughts, beliefs and actions is a psychoanalytical concern.

Faith matters—be it defined as more or less religious, atheist, or else. I hope to have given some ideas on how to explore it further.

Acknowledgements

Everything that develops needs a space where it can do that. The Bielefeld-Chattanooga Research Team, guided by Heinz Streib and Ralph Hood, has offered such a developmental space for many years.

Herbert Will, psychoanalyst in Munich, has given me the opportunity to present suggestions to integrate concepts and methods from psychology of religion and psychoanalysis in the study group he organizes.

Ralph Hood offered me the space of this publication to lay out some ideas and suggestions in more detail and gave valuable encouragement along the way.

I am grateful for all the support and hope that the result is useful.

References

Abu-Raiya, H. (2014). Western psychology and Muslim psychology in dialogue: Comparisons between a Qura'nic theory of personality and Freud's and Jung's ideas. *Journal of Religion and Health*, 53:326–338, DOI 10.1007/s10943-012-9630-9.

Ağılkaya-Şahin, S. (2015). The problem of appropriate psychology of religion measures for non-western Christian samples with respect to the Turkish—Islamic religious landscape. In: Ağılkaya-Sahin, S., Streib, H., Ayten, A. & Hood, R. W. Jr. (eds.) *Psychology of religion in Turkey*. Leiden, The Netherlands: Brill, 65–104.

Allen, J. G., Fonagy, P., & Bateman, A. W. (2008). *Mentalizing in clinical practice*. Arlington: American Psychiatric Publishing.

Altemeyer, B and Hunsberger, B. (1997). *Amazing conversions: Why some turn to faith and other abandon religion.* Amherst, NY: Prometheus Books.

Anders, G. (1989). *Lieben gestern. Notizen zu einer Geschichte des Fühlens.* (Loving yesterday. Notes for a history of emotions). München: C. H. Beck.

Anders, G. (1985). *Die Antiquiertheit des Menschen. Über die Seele im Zeitalter der zweiten industriellen Revolution.* (The Obsolescence of Man. The soul in the age of the second industrial revolution). München: Beck.

Aten, J. D., O'Grady, K. A. & Worthington, E. L. (2012). The psychology of religion and spirituality for clinicians. An introduction. In J. D. Aten, K. A. O'Grady & E. L. Worthington (eds.), *The psychology of religion and spirituality for clinicians: using research in your practice* 1.12. New York, London: Routledge.

Aygün, A. (2010). Religiöse Sozialisation und Entwicklung bei muslimischen Jugendlichen in Deutschland und in der Türkei: Empirische Analyse und religionspädagogische Herausforderungen [Religious socialization and development of Muslim adults in Germany and Turkey: Empirical analysis and challenges in religious education]. Bielefeld: University Bielefeld.

Badcock, C. R. (1980). *The psychoanalysis of culture.* Oxford: Basil Blackwell.

Baltes, P. B., Lindenberger, U. & Staudinger, U. M. (2006). Lifespan theory in developmental psychology. In R. Lerner & W. Damon (eds), *Handbook of child psychology.* Vol. I. Theoretical models of human development. Hoboken: Wiley.

Barrett, J. (2017). Could we advance the science of religion (better) without the concept of religion? *Religion, Brain and Behavior*, Vol 7 Issue 4, 282–284.

Bartlett, F. C. (1950). *Religion as experience, belief, action.* London, New York, Toronto: Oxford University Press.

Beit-Hallahmi, B. (2015). *Psychological perspectives on religion and religiosity.* London / New York: Routledge.

Bering, J. M. (2006). The cognitive psychology of belief in the supernatural. *Scientific American*, 94, 142–149.

Bloom, P. (2007). Religion is natural. *Developmental Science* 10:1, pp. 147–151. DOI: 10.1111/j.1467-7687.2007.00577.x.

Bowlby, J. (1940). The influence of early environment in the development of neurosis and neurotic character. *International Journal of Psycho-Analysis*, XXI, 1–25.

Bowlby, J. (1969). *Attachment and Loss*, vol. I: Attachment. London: Hogarth Press.

Bretherton, I. (1992). The origins of attachment theory: John Bowlby and Mary Ainsworth. *Developmental Psychology*, 28, 759–775.

Bretherton, I. & Munholland, K. A. (2008). Internal working models in attachment relationships: A construct revisited. In: Cassidy, J. & Shaver, P. R. (eds.), *Handbook of attachment: Theory, research and clinical applications.* 2nd edition. New York: Guilford Press.

Bullik, R., Keller, B. & Swanson, S. (in preparation). Entering old age and becoming wise: The case of Sophia. In Streib, H., Keller, B., Bullik, R., Silver, C. F. & Hood, R. W. (eds.) *Deconversion revisited. Longitudinal biographical analyses ten years later.*

Butenaite, J. (2019). *Roman Catholic faith of older people: Types, expressions in the life course and its impact for psychological resilience.* Doctoral Thesis, Social Sciences, Psychology, Mykolo Romero Universtitetas.

Cantwell Smith, W. (1963). *The meaning and end of religion.* Minneapolis: Fortress Press 1991.

Cantwell Smith, W. (1979). *Faith and belief. Princeton*: Princeton University Press.

Chen, Z., Hood, R. W., Yang, L. & Watson, P. J. (2011). Mystical experience among Tibetan Buddhists: The Common Core Thesis revisited. *Journal for the Scientific Study of Religion* 50(2):328–338.

Cohler, B. J. (1982). Personal narrative and life course. In P. Baltes & O. G. Brim (eds.), *Life span development and behavior* (Vol. 4, pp. 205–241). New York, NY: Academic Press.

Costa, P. T. & McCrae, R. R. (1985). *Revised NEO Personality Inventory (NEO PI-R) and NEO Five-Factor-Inventory (NEO-FFI).* Professional Manual, Odessa.

DeYoung, C. G. (2006). Higher-order factors of the Big Five in a multi-informant sample. *Journal of Personality and Social Psychology*, 91, 1138–1151.

DeYoung, C. G., Peterson, J. B., & Higgins, D. M. (2002). Higher-order factors of the Big Five predict conformity: Are there neuroses of health? *Personality and Individual Differences*, 33, 533–553.

Eigen, M. (1998). *The psychoanalytic mystic.* London and New York: Free Association Books.

Fonagy, P. (2008). The mentalization-focussed approach to social development. In Busch, F. N. (ed.) Mentalization. Theoretical considerations, research findings, and clinical implications. New York/London: The Analytic Press.

Fonagy P, Campbell C. (2015). Bad blood revisited: attachment and psychoanalysis. *British Journal of Psychotherapy* 31:229–50.

Fonagy P. Gergely G. Jurist E. Target M (2002). *Affect regulation, mentalization, and the development of the self.* New York. NY; Other Press.

Fonagy, P., Luyten, P., Moulton-Perkins, A., Lee, Y. W., Warren, F., Howard, S., et al. (2016). Development and validation of a self-report measure of mentalizing: The Reflective Functioning Questionnaire. *PLoS ONE.* 11(7):e0158678. doi: 10.1371/journal.pone.0158678.

Fonagy, P., Luyten, P., Allison, E. & Campbell, C. (2017). What we have changed our minds about: Part 1. Borderline personality disorder as a limitation of resilience. *Emotion Dysregulation* 4:11. DOI 10.1186/s40479-017-0061-9.

Fonagy, P., Luyten, P., Allison, E. & Campbell, C. (2019). Mentalizing, epistemic trust and the phenomenology of psychotherapy. *Psychopathology.* DOI: 10.1159/000501526.

Fonagy, P., & Target, M. (1997). Attachment and reflective function: Their role in self-organization. *Development and Psychopathology*, 9, 679–700.

Fonagy, P. & Target, M. (2003). *Psychoanalytic theories. Perspectives from developmental psychopathology*. Chapter 12: Fonagy and Target's model of mentalization 270–283. London / Philadelphia: Whurr Publishers Ltd.

Fonagy, P. & Target, M. (2007). Playing with reality IV. A theory of external reality rooted in intersubjectivity. *International Journal of Psychoanalysis* 88: 917–937.

Fowler, J. W. (1981). *Stages of Faith. The psychology of human development and the quest for meaning*. San Francisco: Harper & Row.

Fowler, J. W. (1987). *Faith development and pastoral care*. Philadephia: Fortress Press.

Fowler, J. W. (1996). *Faithful change. The personal and public challenges of postmodern life*. Nashville: Abingdon Press.

Fowler, James W. (2004). 'Faith development at 30: Naming the challenges of faith in a new millennium, *Religious Education*, 99:4, 405–421. DOI.10.1080/00344080490513036.

Freud S (1895). Studies on hysteria. In: Strachey J (ed. and trans.) *The standard edition of the complete psychological works of Sigmund Freud*, vol 2. Hogarth Press, London.

Freud, S. (1919). *Totem and Taboo. Resemblances between the psychic lives of savages and neurotics*. Translator: A. A. Brill. London: George Routledge & Sons, limited.

Freud, S. (1921). Postscript Group psychology and the analysis of the Ego. *The standard edition of the complete psychological writings of Sigmund Freud*, Vol. 18 (pp. 69–143). London: Hogarth.

Freud, S. (1927a). *The future of an illusion. The standard edition of the complete psychological writings of Sigmund Freud*, Vol. 21 (pp. 3–56). London: Hogarth.

Freud, S. (1927b). Postscript to the question of lay analysis. *Standard Edition* 20: 251–258.

Freud, S. (1930). Civilization and its discontents. *The Standard Edition 1*, reprint New York: Norton 1989.

Fuller, R. C. (2013). *The body of faith. A biological history of religion in America*. Chicago: the University of Chicago Press.

Gooren, H. (2011). Deconversion: Qualitative and quantitative results from cross-cultural research in Germany and the United States: A review essay. *Pastoral Psychology*, 60: 609–617. DOI: https://doi.org/10.1007/s11089-011-0369-0.

Granqvist, P. (2006). On the relation between secular and divine relationships: An emerging attachment perspective and a critique of the "depth" approaches. *The International Journal for the Psychology of Religion*, 16(1), 1–18.

Granqvist, P. (2010). Religion as attachment: The Godin award lecture. *Archive for the Psychology of Religion*, 32, 5–24.

Granqvist, P. (2020). *Attachment in religion and spirituality: A wider view*. New York: Guilford.

Granqvist, P., Fransson, M., & Hagekull, B. (2009). Disorganized attachment, absorption, and New Age spirituality—A mediational model. *Attachment and Human Development*, 11, 385–403.

Granqvist, P., Hagekull, B., & Ivarsson, T. (2012). Disorganized attachment promotes mystical experiences via a propensity for alterations in consciousness (Absorption). *The International Journal for the Psychology of Religion*, 22, 180–197.

Granqvist, P., Ivarsson, T., Broberg, A. G., & Hagekull, B. (2007). Examining relations between attachment, religiosity, and New Age spirituality using the Adult Attachment Interview. *Developmental Psychology*, 43, 590–601.

Granqvist, P. & Kirkpatrick, L. A. (2016). Attachment and religious representations and behavior. In Cassidy, J. & Shaver, Ph. R (eds.) *Handbook of Attachment: Theory, Research, and Clinical Applications,* New York: Guilford. Pp. 917–940.

Grotstein, J. (1990). Introduction. In M. L. Little *Psychotic anxieties and containment: A personal record of an analysis with Winnicott*. Northvale: Aronson.

Grünbaum, A. (1984). *The foundations of psychoanalysis: A philosophical critique*. Berkeley: University of California Press.

Grünbaum, A. (1987). Psychoanalysis and theism. *The Monist*, 70, 152–192.

Habermas, J. (2019). *Auch eine Geschichte der Philosophie. Band 2 Vernünftige Freiheit. Spuren des Diskurses über Glauben und Wissen*. (Also a history of philosophy. Rational freedom. Traces of the discourse on faith and knowledge). Frankfurt: Suhrkamp.

Habermas, T. (2007). How to tell a life: The development of the cultural concept of biography across the lifespan. *Journal of Cognition and Development*, 8, 1–31.

Habermas, T. (2010). Autobiographical reasoning: Arguing and narrating from a biographical perspective. *New Directions for Child and Adolescent Development*, 131, 1–17.

Habermas, T. & Berger, N. (2011). Retelling everyday emotional events: Condensation, distancing, and closure. *Cognition & Emotion*, 25 (2), 206–219.

Hall, T. W. (2007). Psychoanalysis, attachment, and spirituality Part I: The emergence of two relational traditions. *Journal of Psychology and Theology* 35, 1, 14–28.

Hanegraaff, W. J. (2019): Imagining the future study of religion and spirituality. *Religion*, DOI: 10.1080/0048721X.2019.1681103.

Hare-Mustin, R. T. (1983). An appraisal of the relationship between women and psychotherapy: 80 years after the case of Dora. *American Psychologist*, 38(5), 593–601. https://doi.org/10.1037/0003-066X.38.5.593.

Harrison, Peter (1990). *'Religion' and the religions in the English Enlightenment*, Cambridge: Cambridge University Press.

Hartmann, H. (1958). *Ego Psychology and the problem of adaptation.* New York: International University Press.

Herzog, Dagmar (2017). *Cold War Freud. Psychoanalysis in an age of catastrophes.* Cambridge: Cambridge University Press.

Hoffman, M. T. (2011). *Toward mutual recognition. Relational psychoanalysis and the Christian narrative.* New York, London: Routledge. (Relational Perspectives Book Series, Vol. 48).

Hoffmann, L. & Walach, H. (2011). Spirituality and religiosity in psychotherapy—A representative survey among German psychotherapists. Psychotherapy Research, 21:2, 179–192, http://dx.doi.org/10.1080/10503307.2010.536595.

Holliman, P. (2002). Religious experience as selfobject experience. 193–215. In A. Goldberg (ed.) *Postmodern Self Psychology. Progress in Self Psychology,* Volume 18. Hillsdale, NJ: The Analytic Press Inc.

Hood, R. W. Jr. (1997). Psychoanalysis and fundamentalism: Lessons from a feminist critique of Freud. In J. L. Jacobs & D. Capps (eds.), *Religion, society, and psychoanalysis* (pp. 42–57). Boulder, Colorado: Westview Press.

Hood, R. W. Jr., Hill, P. C. & Spilka, B. (2018). *The psychology of religion. An empirical approach.* New York, London: The Guilford Press.

Hood, R., & Belzen, J. A. (2005). Research methods in the psychology of religion. In R. F. Paloutzian & C. L. Park (eds.), *Handbook of the psychology of religion and spirituality* (pp. 62–79). New York/London: Guilford.

Hood, R. W. Jr., Hill, P. C. & Williamson, W. Paul (2005). *The psychology of religious fundamentalism.* New York / London: The Guilford Press.

Hopkins, E. W. (1923). *Origin and evolution of religion.* New Haven, CT: Yale University Press.

Jacobs, T. (1986). On countertransference enactments. *Journal of the American Psychoanalytic Association,* 34:289–307.

James, W. (1912). The varieties of religious experience. Oxford: Oxford University Press. (Original work published 1901–2).

Jensen, U. (2019). *Wie die Couch nach Kalkutta kam. Eine Globalgeschichte der frühen Psychoanalyse* (How the couch got to Calcutta. A global history of early psychoanalysis) Frankfurt/Main: Suhrkamp.

Jones, J. W. (1996). *Religion and psychology in transition. Psychoanalysis, feminism, and theology.* New Haven/London: Yale University Press.

Josselson, R. (2009). The present of the past: Dialogues with memory over time. *Journal of Personality* 77:3, 647–668.

Kächele, H., Albani, C. & Pokorny, D. (2015). From psychoanalytic narrative case study to quantitative single case research. In O. Gelo & A. Pritz (eds.) *Psychotherapy research: General issues, outcome and process,* Vienna: Springer, (pp. 367–379).

Kauders, A. D. (2014). *Der Freud-Komplex. Eine Geschichte der Psychoanalyse in Deutschland* (The Freud-Complex. A history of psychoanalysis in Germany). Berlin: Berlin Verlag.

Kegan, R. (1982). *The evolving self. Problem and process in human development.* Cambridge: Harvard University Press.

Keller, B. (2008). Toward a multidimensional conception of Faith Development: Deconversion narratives in biographical context. In J. A. Belzen & A. Geels (eds.) *Autobiography and the psychological study of religious lives.* Amsterdam, New York: Rodopi, 75–93.

Keller, B., Klein, C., Hood, R. W. & Streib, H. (2013). Deconversion and religious or spiritual transformation. In: *Constructs of meaning and religious transformation. Current issues in the psychology of religion.* Westerink, H. (ed.); Religion and transformation in contemporary European society, 4 (pp. 119–139). Göttingen: V&R unipress / Vienna University Press.

Keller, B., Coleman, T. J., & Silver, C. F. (2016). Narrative reconstruction and content analysis in the interpretation of "spiritual" biographical trajectories for case studies. In H. Streib & R. W. Hood (eds.), *Semantics and psychology of spirituality. A cross-cultural Analysis* (pp. 251–271). Cham, Heidelberg, New York, Dordrecht, London: Springer International Publishing Switzerland.

Keller, B., Klein, C., & Streib, H. (2013). Das Interview zur Glaubensentwicklung: Zur Exploration von Spiritualität im psychotherapeutischen Setting. *Spiritual Care*, 2, 35–43 (The faith development interview: On exploring spirituality in psychotherapeutic settings).

Keller, B. & Streib, H. (2013). Faith development, religious styles and biographical narratives: Methodological perspectives. *Journal of Empirical Theology*, 26, 1–21, online: http://pub.uni-bielefeld.de/download/2555007/2580429.

Keller, B., Streib, H. & Hood, Ralph W. (2016). Redrawing the map: Varieties of "spiritual," "religious" and "secular" lives. In Streib H. & Hood R. W. (eds.) (2016) Semantics and psychology of spirituality. A Cross-cultural analysis. Cham: Springer. https://doi.org/10.1007/978-3-319-21245-6.

Keller, B., Bullik, R., Klein, C. & Swanson, S. B. (2018). Profiling atheist world views in different cultural contexts: Developmental trajectories and accounts. *Psychology of Religion and Spirituality* 10(3): 229–243. http://dx.doi.org/10.1037/rel0000212.

Kind, J. (2017). *Das Tabu. Was Psychoanalytiker nicht denken dürfen, sich aber trauen sollten.* (The taboo. What psychoanalysts must not but should dare to think). Stuttgart: Klett-Cotta.

Kirkpatrick, L. A. (1992). An attachment-theory approach to the psychology of religion. *The International Journal for the Psychology of Religion*, 2, 3–28.

Kirkpatrick, L. A. (2005). *Attachment, evolution, and the psychology of religion.* New York, NY: Guilford Press.

Koschorke, A. (2012). *Wahrheit und Erfindung. Grundzüge einer Allgemeinen Erzähltheorie*. Frankfurt/M. American translation (2018): Fact and fiction. Elements of a general theory of narrative. Translated by Joel Golb. Berlin Boston: Walter De Gruyter.

Krause, N. (2016). Aging. In D. Yamane (ed.), *Handbook of religion and society*, Handbooks of sociology and social research (pp. 263–280). Springer International Publishing Switzerland. DOI 10.1007/978-3-319-31395-5_14.

Labov, W. & Waletzky, J. (1967). Narrative analysis: Oral versions of personal experience. In J. Helms (Ed.), *Essays on the Verbal and Visual Arts* (pp. 12–44). Seattle: University of Washington Press.

Lamiell, J. T. (1981). Toward an idiothetic psychology of personality. *American Psychologist*, 36, 276–289.

Lamiell, J. T. (2019). *Psychology's misuse of statistics and persistent dismissal of its critics*. Palgrave Studies in the Theory and History of Psychology. Cham: Springer Nature.

Leichsenring, F., Abbass, A., Hilsenroth, M. J., Luyten, P., Munder, T., Rabung, S. & Steinert, C. (2018). "Gold standards," plurality and monocultures: The need for diversity in psychotherapy. *Frontiers in Psychiatry* 9:159. doi: 10.3389/fpsyt.2018.00159.

Leuzinger-Bohleber, M., Stuhr, U. Rüger, B. & Beutel, M. (2003). How to study the 'quality of psychoanalytic treatments' and their long-term effects on patients' well-being: A representative, multi-perspective follow-up study. *International Journal of Psychoanalysis*, 84: 263–290.

Leuzinger-Bohleber, M., Fischmann, T. (2006). Research subcommittee for conceptual research of the International Psychoanalytical Association. What is conceptual research in psychoanalysis? *International Journal of Psychoanalysis*, 87, 355–86.

Lev, G. (2018). Poetics of reconcilement: Psychoanalysis and dilemmas of faith. *Psychoanalytic Psychology*, 35, No. 1, 38–45.

Loewald, H. W. (1970). Psychoanalytic theory and the psychoanalytic process. The *Psychoanalytic Study of the Child*, 25, 45–68.

Loewald, H. (1978). Psychoanalysis and the history of the individual. New Haven, CT: Yale University Press.

Luyten, P. & Corveleyn, J. (2007). Attachment and religion: The need to leave our secure base: A comment on the discussion between Granqvist, Rizzuto, and Wulff, *The International Journal for the Psychology of Religion*, 17(2), 81–97.

Main, M., Hesse, E. & Hesse, S. (2011). Attachment theory and research: Overview with suggested applications to child custody. *Family Court Review* 49: 426–63.

Main, M., Kaplan, N. & Cassidy, J. (1985). Security in infancy, childhood, and adulthood: A move to the level of representation. *Monographs of the Society for Research in Child Development* 50: 66–104.

Makari, G. (2008). *Revolution in mind. The creation of psychoanalysis.* New York: HarperCollins.

McAdams, D. P. (1993). *The stories we live by: Personal myths and the making of the self.* New York: Guilford Press 1997.

McAdams, D. & Albaugh, M. (2008a). The redemptive self, generativity, and American Christians at midlife: Explorations of the life stories of evangelical and mainline protestants. In J. A. Belzen & A. Geels (eds.). *Autobiography and the psychological study of religious lives.* Amsterdam, New York: Rodopi, 255–286. DOI: 10.1163/9789042029125_012.

McAdams, D. & Albaugh, M. (2008b). What if there were no God? Politically conservative and liberal Christians imagine their lives without faith. *Journal of Research in Personality* 42(6): 1668–1672. DOI: 10.1016/j.jrp.2008.07.013.

McAdams, D. P. & Olson, B. D. (2010). Personality development: Continuity and change over the life course. *Annual Review of Psychology*, 517–542.

McAdams, D. P., & de St. Aubin, E. (1992). A theory of generativity and its assessment through self-report, behavioral acts, and narrative themes in autobiography. *Journal of Personality and Social Psychology*, 62, 1003–1015.

McCauley, R. N. (2011). *Why religion is natural and science is not.* New York, NY: Oxford University Press.

McCrae, R. R. & Costa, P. T. (1987). Validation of the Five-Factor Model of Personality across instruments and observers, *Journal of Personality and Social Psychology* 52, 81–90.

Meissner, W. W. (2001). So help me God. Do I help God or does God help me? In S. Akhtar & H. Parens (eds.). *Does God help?* Lanham: Jason Aronson (pp. 75–126).

Meissner, W. W. (1984). *Psychoanalysis and religious experience.* New Haven: Yale University Press.

Merkur, D. (2010). Wilfred R. Bion's transformations of O. Ch 9 of *Explorations of the psychoanalytic mystics*, Leiden: Brill (pp. 227–256).

Merleau-Ponty, M. (1988). *Merleau-Ponty à la Sorbonne. Résumède cours 1949–1952.* Paris: Edition Cynara.

Mitchell, S. A. (1999). Attachment theory and the psychoanalytic tradition. Reflections on human relationality. *Psychoanalytic Dialogues*, 9(1) 85–107.

Mitchell, S. A. (2000). *Relationality: From attachment to intersubjectivity.* Hillsdale, NJ-London: The Analytic Press.

Noam, G. G. (1990). *Beyond Freud and Piaget: Biographical worlds—Interpersonal self.* In T. Wren (ed.), The moral domain (pp. 360–399). Cambridge, MA: MIT Press.

Orange, D. M. (2017). *Climate crisis, psychoanalysis, and radical ethics.* London, UK: Routledge.

Ostov, I. (2007). *Spirit, mind and brain. A psychoanalytic examination of spirituality and religion.* New York: Columbia University Press.

Özışık, S. (2015). *Intergenerational changes in the religiosity of Turkish Islamic immigrants in contemporary Germany*. A qualitative analysis using the Faith Development Interview. Dissertation submitted to the Faculty of History, Philosophy, and Theology, Department of Theology, Bielefeld University.

Pérez, S. & Vallières, F. (2019). How do religious people become atheists? Applying a Grounded Theory approach to propose a model of deconversion. *Secularism and Nonreligion*, 8: 3, pp. 1–14. DOI: https://doi.org/10.5334/snr.108.

Pine, F. (1988). The four psychologies of psychoanalysis and their place in clinical work. *Journal of the American Psychoanalytic Association*, 36, 571–596.

Prickett, S. (2002). *Narrative, religion, and science. Fundamentalism versus irony 1700–1999*. Cambridge: Cambridge University Press.

Ricoeur, P. (1992). *Oneself as another.* Chicago: University of Chicago Press. (Original work published 1990).

Rizzuto, A.-M. (1979). *The birth of the living God. A psychoanalytic study*. Chicago, London: University of Chicago Press.

Rizzuto A.-M. (2006). Discussion of Granqvist's article "On the relation between secular and divine relationships: An emerging attachment perspective and a critique of the 'depth' approaches" *The International Journal for the Psychology of Religion*, 16(1), 19–28.

Ryff, C. D. (1989). Happiness is everything, or is it? Explorations on the meaning of psychological well-being, *Journal of Personality and Social Psychology* 57, 1069–1081.

Saroglou, V. (2002a). Religion and the five factors of personality: A meta-analytic review. *Personality and Individual Differences*, 32, 15–25.

Saroglou, V. (2002b). Beyond dogmatism: The need for closure related to religion. *Mental Health, Religion and Culture*, 5, 183–194.

Schaap-Jonker, H. & Corveleyn, J. (2014). Mentalizing and religion: a promising combination for psychology of religion, illustrated by the case of prayer. *Archive for the Psychology of Religion* 36. 1–20. DOI: 10.1163/15736121-12341292.

Schiff, B. (2014). Introduction: Development's story in time and place. In B. Schiff (ed.), *Rereading personal narrative and life course. New directions for child and adolescent development*, 145, 1–13.

Schleiermacher, F. D. E. (1799). Über die Religion. Reden an die Gebildeten unter ihren Verächtern in: *Kritische Gesamtausgabe, Bd. I/2: Schriften aus der Berliner Zeit 1769–1799*, hg. v. Günter Meckenstock, Verlag Walter de Gruyter, Berlin/New York, S. 212. (On Religion: Speeches to its cultured despisers. In Schleiermacher: Critical complete edition).

Schur, M. (1982). *Sigmund Freud*. Frankfurt: Suhrkamp. (orig 1972 Freud: Living and dying, New York: International Universities Press).

Schwarz, N. & Hippler, H.-J. (1987). What response scales may tell your respondents: Informative functions of response alternatives. In: Hippler H.-J., Schwarz N.,

Sudman S. (eds.). *Social information processing and survey methodology. Recent research in psychology*. New York: Springer, https://doi.org/10.10007/978/1-4612-4798-2-9.

Shafranske, E. P. (1985). Freudian theory and religious experience. In R. W. Hood, Jr. (ed.), *Handbook of religious experience* (pp. 200–230). Birmingham, AL: Religious Education Press.

Simmonds, J. G. (2006). The oceanic feeling and a sea change. Historical challenges to reductionist attitudes to religion and spirit from within psychoanalysis. *Psychoanalytic Psychology* 23, No. 1, 128–142.

Sorenson, R. L. (2004). *Minding Spirituality*. Hillsdale/NJ: The Analytic Press.

Stern, D. N. (1985). *The interpersonal world of the infant*. New York: Basic Books.

Stern, W. (1911). *Die Differentielle Psychologie in ihren methodischen Grundlagen* [Methodological foundations of differential psychology]. Leipzig: Barth.

Stern, W. (1930). *Eindrücke von der amerikanischen Psychologie. Bericht über eine Kongreßreise* [Impressions of American psychology: Report after travel to a conference]. Zeitschrift für Pädagogische Psychologie, experimentelle Pädagogik und Jugendkundliche Forschung, 31, 43–51 and 65–72.

Streib, H. (2001). Faith development theory revisited: The religious styles perspective. *The International Journal for the Psychology of Religion*, 11, 143–158.

Streib, H. (2003). Religion as a question of style: Revising the structural differentiation of religion from the perspective of the analysis of the contemporary pluralistic-religious situation. *International Journal for Practical Theology*, 7, 1–22.

Streib, H. (2005). Faith Development research revisited: Accounting for diversity in structure, content, and narrativity of faith. *The International Journal for the Psychology of Religion*, 15 (2).

Streib, H. (2011). Conceptualizing and measuring religious development in terms of religious styles and schemata. New considerations and results. Paper for the Conference „Psychologie du développement religieux: questions classiques et perspectives contemporaires" 2010–05–27 in Lausanne.

Streib, H. (2013). Conceptualisation et mesure du développement religieux en termes de schémas et de styles religieux—Résultats et nouvelles considérations. In P.-Y. Brandt & J. M. Day (eds.), *Psychologie du développement religieux: questions classiques et perspectives contemporaines* (pp. 39–76). Geneva: Labor et Fides.

Streib, H., Chen, Z. J. & Hood, R. W. (2019). Categorizing people by their preference for religious styles: Four types derived from evaluation of Faith Development Interviews. *The International Journal for the Psychology of Religion*: 1–16. https://doi.org/10.1080/10508619.2019.1664213.

Streib, H., & Hood, R. W. (2013). Modeling the religious field: Religion, spirituality, mysticism and related world views. *Implicit Religion*, 16, 137–155. doi:10.1558/imre.v16i2.137.

Streib, H., Hood, R. W., Keller, B., Csöff, R. M. &, Silver, C. F. (2009). *Deconversion: qualitative and quantitative results from cross-cultural research in Germany and the United States of America*. Research in contemporary religion; 5. Göttingen: Vandenhoeck und Ruprecht.

Streib H. & Hood, R. W. (2016). *Semantics and psychology of spirituality. A Cross-cultural analysis*. Cham: Springer. https://doi.org/10.1007/978-3-319-21245-6.

Streib, H., Hood, R. W., & Klein, C. (2010). The religious schema scale: Construction and initial validation of a quantitative measure for religious styles. *The International Journal for the Psychology of Religion*, 20, 151–172. https://doi.org/10.1080/10508619.2010.481223.

Streib, H. & Keller, B. (2018). *Manual for the assessment of religious styles in faith development interviews* (Fourth, revised edition of the manual for faith development research) Bielefeld: Universität Bielefeld, Center for Biographical Studies in Contemporary Religion. PUB: https://pub.uni-bielefeld.de/record/2920987. DOI: 10.4119/unibi/2920987.

Streib, H., Keller, B., Bullik, R., Silver, C. F. & Hood, R. W. (In preparation). *Deconversion revisited. Longitudinal biographical analyses ten years later*.

Streib, H., Klein, C., Keller B. & Hood, R. W. (In Press). The mysticism scale as measure for subjective spirituality: New results with Hood's M-Scale and the development of a short form. In: Ai, A. L., Harris, K. A. & Wink, P. (eds); *Assessing spirituality and religion in a diversified world: Beyond the mainstream perspective*. New York: Springer. PUB: https://pub.uni-bielefeld.de/record/2930261.

Tarar, A. H., Hassan, S. S. & Keller, B. (2017). Muslim Faith in Pakistan: A Faith-Development view on fundamentalist to mature orientations. *Archive for the Psychology of Religion* 39(1): 27–60. PUB: https://pub.uni-bielefeld.de/record/2916593. DOI: 10.1163/15736121-12341334. WoS: 000403328400002.

Target, M. & Fonagy, P. (1996). Playing with reality II. The development of psychic reality from a theoretical perspective. *International Journal of Psycho-Analysis*, 77, 459–479.

Tylor, E. B. (1873). *Primitive culture* (Vol. 2). London, UK: Murray.

Vermote, R. (2019). *Reading Bion*. The New Library of Psychoanalysis Teaching Series, edited by Dana Birksted-Breen. London / New York: Routledge.

Whitebook, J. (2014). "Imagine". Zur Verteidigung des Säkularismus in der Psychoanalyse. *Psyche—Zeitschrift für Psychoanalyse und ihre Anwendungen* 68, 1167–1195. („Imagine"—Defending psychoanalytic secularism).

Will, H. (2017). Religiöse Erfahrung als Transgression. Ein Gedicht Edith Jacobsons aus nationalsozialistischer Haft als Beispiel (Religious experience as transgression. With reference to a poem written by Edith Jacobson in Nazi detention). *Psyche—Zeitschrift für Psychoanalyse und ihre Anwendungen* 71, 235–259.

Will, H. (2014a). Vom Niedergang der Weltanschauungen. Freuds Atheismus im Kontext betrachtet. *Psyche—Zeitschrift für Psychoanalyse und ihre Anwendungen*, 68, 1–30. (The decline of worldviews. Freud's atheism in context).

Will, H. (2014b). *Freuds Atheismus im Widerspruch. Freud, Weber und Wittgenstein im Konflikt zwischen säkularem Denken und Religion*. (Freud's atheism in contradiction. Freud, Weber and Wittgenstein in conflict between secular thinking and religion). Stuttgart: Kohlhammer.

Wimmer, H. & Perner, J. (1983). Beliefs about beliefs: Representation and constraining function of wrong beliefs in young children's understanding of deception. In: *Cognition* 13, 1, 103–128, doi:10.1016/0010-0277(83)90004-5.

Windelband, W. (1894/1998). History and natural science (J. T. Lamiell, Trans.). *Theory and Psychology*, 8, 6–22.

Winnicott, D. W. (1953.). Transitional objects and transitional phenomena. *International Journal of Psychoanalysis*, 34:2, 89–97.

Winnicott, D. W. (1971). Playing and reality. New York: Routledge.

Wulff, D. M. (2006). How attached should we be to Attachment Theory? *The International Journal for the Psychology of Religion*, 16(1), 29–36.

Xygalatas, D. (2016). Cognitive science of religion. In D. A. Leeming (Ed.), Encyclopedia of psychology and religion (pp. 343–347). Boston, MA: Springer.

www.ingramcontent.com/pod-product-compliance
Lightning Source LLC
LaVergne TN
LVHW102228300926
849160LV00005B/65